The Global City Debate Reconsidered

The Global City Debate Reconsidered

Economic Globalization in Contemporary Dutch Cities

Jeroen van der Waal

Routledge
Taylor & Francis Group
LONDON AND NEW YORK

First published in 2015 by Amsterdam University Press Ltd.

Published 2025 by Routledge
4 Park Square, Milton Park, Abingdon, Oxon OX14 4RN
605 Third Avenue, New York, NY 10158

Routledge is an imprint of the Taylor & Francis Group, an informa business

ISBN: 9789089647603 (hbk)
ISBN: 9781041188018 (pbk)
ISBN: 9781003706304 (ebk)
NUR 903

Cover design: Maedium, Utrecht

DOI: 10.5117/9789089647603

For Amy, with love

Contents

Acknowledgements

Doing sociological research is anything but an individual endeavour. I am therefore privileged to have been surrounded by excellent sociologists for quite some time now. Some of these colleagues deserve special mention for their valuable contributions to the development of my sociological imagination and research skills, both of which were needed to write this book; Stef Aupers, Peter Achterberg, Jack Burgers, Dick Houtman, and Willem de Koster: I am very grateful to you. Our countless and entertaining discussions on sociological research have improved this book's quality enormously. Any mistakes and shortcomings that remain are all mine.

This book is part of my line of research into urban sociology, which began almost a decade ago with the start of my PhD project. As a consequence, parts of the book resonate with earlier publications, most notably a set of research articles contained in the journal *Urban Studies*. I am grateful to Sage for permitting me to re-use parts of the following articles: 'Post-Industrialisation, Job Opportunities and Ethnocentrism. A Comparison of Twenty-two Dutch Urban Economies' (2011) and 'Cultural Amenities and Unemployment in Dutch Cities. Disentangling a Consumerist and Productivist Explanation for Less-Educated Urbanites' Varying Unemployment Levels across Urban Economies' (2013) for Chapter 3; 'Foreign Direct Investments and International Migration to Dutch Cities' (2013) for Chapter 4; and 'Post-Industrialisation, Immigration, and Unemployment. How and Why the Impact of Immigration on Unemployment Differs between Dutch Cities' (2012) for Chapter 5. I am also grateful to the Netherlands Organization for Scientific Research (NWO) for providing me with the grants that have enabled me to write this book in recent years (grant numbers W 07.68.117.00 and 451-13-005).

Most of all, I would like to thank Amy for all of her love and patience. It is to her that I dedicate this book.

Jeroen van der Waal
Papendrecht, December 2014

1 Introduction

Economic globalization (...) has profoundly altered the social, economic, and political reality of (...) cities. Through the study of the city as one particular site in which global processes take place, I seek to define new concepts useful to understand the intersection of the global and the local in today's world (Sassen, 1994: xiii, preface to Cities in a World Economy).

1.1 Reconsidering the global city debate

This study addresses the global city debate, in which much has been said, but little is known. This debate revolves around the impact of economic globalization on urban labour markets in the advanced economies, and was initiated by Saskia Sassen's global city theoretical framework. This framework was first published in 1991 in *The Global City. New York, London, Tokyo*. However, the arguments from which it was built can be found in earlier work on this subject (Sassen-Koob, 1984a, 1984b, 1985, 1986; Sassen, 1988), and it has remained unchanged to date (Sassen, 2001, 2006a, 2007, 2012). Sassen deemed that the integration of these arguments into an all-encompassing framework was necessary because, as the quote above reveals, the old concepts by which 'sociologists have tended to study cities (...) are no longer sufficient' (Sassen, 1994: xiii) when it comes to understanding the impact of the current phase of economic globalization on the social and economic reality of contemporary cities.

Although this framework was initially formulated to explain how the current phase of economic globalization has altered the economic base and labour markets of New York, London, and Tokyo, as the subtitle reveals, its scope has widened considerably, to say the least. In the first place, the number of global cities has increased from this initial triad to 'about 40' in 2006 (Sassen, 2006a: 142, 2006c: 315), and 'about seventy worldwide' in 2012 (Sassen, 2012: 7). Secondly, and more important for the issue addressed in this study, the global city theoretical framework has now evolved into 'an *analytical construct* that allows one to detect the global as it is filtered through the specifics of a place' (Sassen, 2006c: x; italics added). As such, it has inspired dozens of studies on the impact of economic globalization on hundreds of urban labour markets in the advanced economies, which range from the usual suspects like New York to cities much lower down the urban hierarchy. Although the global city theoretical framework touches on a wide range of issues, these studies, which are part of, and will consequently be referred to in what follows as 'the global city debate', primarily revolve around these central subjects: 1) the impact on labour demand of the alleged urban manifestation of economic globalization, i.e. deindustrialization and the clustering of advanced producer services; and 2) the role that immigration plays in that process. Yet, more than two decades after their initial formulation, these topics are still disputed. Indeed, with closer scrutiny, most of the studies in the global city debate do not really assess the empirical validity of the global city theory, but instead interpret recent urban developments in terms of the theoretical framework of the global city and attribute them to economic globalization.

As we will see in this book, this research practice is problematic; instead of revealing the impact of economic globalization on urban labour markets by systematically scrutinizing theoretical claims on this issue, it boils down to simply reproducing Sassen's global city theory. Moreover, by introducing new interpretations derived from the global city theoretical framework, several studies in the global city debate have caused additional confusion in terms of how economic globalization actually affects urban labour markets. As a result, we do not yet know whether this framework really does allow us to understand the impact of economic globalization on the social and economic realities of cities, as its creator claims. The same, of course, applies to new interpretations of the arguments in this framework that flourish throughout the global city debate, some of which have even evolved to become practically undisputed assumptions.

Although problematic, it is understandable that the standard research practice in the global city debate evolved into merely interpreting urban changes in cities in the advanced economies on the basis of the arguments in the global city theoretical framework. This is because this framework is not formulated as a middle-range theory in the Mertonian sense (Merton, 1959), and does not therefore permit rigorous empirical testing. With this observation, I am not siding with scholars like Smith (1984, 1998, 2001), who claim that the global city theoretical framework is a grand narrative that merely functions as a vessel for legitimizing neo-liberal economic policies that are more or less rendered inevitable due to global economic restructuring. I will nevertheless deal with that argument in the concluding chapter of this study. Instead, my claim is that the global city theoretical framework is not so much a grand narrative, as a 'grand composition': it is a vast framework constructed from a mix of theories, propositions, and expectations. As a result, the empirical validity of the global city theoretical framework as a whole cannot be assessed. This is why, although much has been said in the global city debate, little has been learned about the very issue it addresses: the impact of economic globalization on the social and economic realities of cities.

Looked at in this way, the fact that the global city theoretical framework has been used to interpret developments in dozens of cities is not so much an indicator of its fruitfulness, but the result of its greatest flaw: being a grand composition instead of a middle-range theory. To be clear, in its infant stage a theory is often not fully crystallized into clear testable propositions. It is thus completely understandable that the global city theoretical framework functioned as a mere prism of interpretation in the 1980s and 90s when it was formulated by Sassen, probably inspired by her empirical observations on the globalizing economy and the concomitant economic change in New York. Yet, I would like to argue that by now – more than two decades later – the global city theoretical framework needs to enter the next stage in its scientific life-cycle, in which its explanatory value is systematically and empirically scrutinized by testing the central hypotheses deduced from it.

Such systematic empirical scrutiny of the tenability of the theoretical notions in the global city debate is precisely what this study aims to provide. To be clear, the book does not opt for two other approaches that can be found in the urban studies literature when it comes to understanding the empirical world by reducing its complexity into concepts and theories. Firstly, this study will *not* provide a more encompassing historical account of the rise and nature of capitalist production, and the role that globalization and cities play therein, as can most notably be found in the Marxist literature that is often self-labelled as 'political economy literature' (cf. Christophers, 2001). Such an approach has its merits, but has aims other than testing the empirical tenability of theoretical notions. The second approach that will explicitly *not* be applied here is that of understanding empirical phenomena by comparing the impact of an inventory of explanations relevant to the issue at hand. This approach can be very productive when the aim is to produce a more complete picture of the phenomenon under study if it is limited to utilizing fully-developed explanations that have already proved their empirical merit. However, the theoretical notions in the global city debate are clearly not yet at that stage of their life-cycle, as outlined above. Scrutinizing their empirical validity, therefore, calls for the approach applied here: systematically deducing hypotheses from theoretical notions, and subsequently testing them so as to 1) uncover whether they have empirical validity and, if so, 2) establish the range of their explanatory value. This is all the more relevant because each theoretical notion in the global city debate builds on the assumption that the other theoretical notions in that debate are empirically valid. As a result, if one of these notions does not hold true empirically, this, almost by definition, invalidates the others.

The central aim of this book is thus: *to assess whether the theoretical notions in the global city theoretical framework and the global city debate help us to understand the impact of the current phase of economic globalization on the social and economic realities of cities.* To achieve this aim, six research questions call for an answer. The first five address central issues in the global city debate, which will be examined in Section 1.2. Nevertheless, more needs to be done to achieve an understanding of the impact of the current phase of economic globalization on the social and economic realities of cities. In the globalization literature at large, there is one debate that revolves around that impact, and which has been overlooked in the global city theoretical framework. As a result, its main issue remains unassessed in the global city debate. However, as we will see, this is highly relevant for a debate that concerns the impact of economic globalization on urban labour markets, and will therefore be addressed in Section 1.3.

1.2 Scrutinizing the global city debate: major issues

1.2.1 The changing economic base of cities

The global city theoretical framework asserts that the so-called 'new international division of labour' (NIDL) is largely responsible for the changing economic base of cities in the advanced economies (Sassen-Koob, 1984a, 1984b, 1985, 1986; Sassen, 1988, 1991, 2001, 2006a, 2012). In particular, it claims that, with the help of the deregulation of international markets and information and communication technology, previously vertically-integrated firms in the advanced economies fragmented their production processes. The purpose of this 'vertical disintegration' was to relocate parts of the production process to places where production costs can be minimized. It goes without saying that for many parts of this process, such conditions can be found outside the advanced economies in so-called 'low-wage countries', which are also referred to as 'newly-industrializing countries' (NICs).

According to the global city theoretical framework, this outsourcing led to globally scattered production processes, hence the new international division of labour, which induced a twofold change in the economic base of cities in the advanced economies, especially the global cities: deindustrialization and the clustering of advanced producer services. When it comes to the first of these changes, a large part of urban employment was industrial until the 1970s. However, since then the employment share of industry has steadily declined due to the outsourcing of industrial production to low-wage countries. In terms of the second change, the global production chains that resulted from this outsourcing need to be centrally managed by the headquarters of multinational corporations that are still located in or near to cities in the advanced economies.

As the management of a globally-dispersed production process is too complex to be dealt with by these headquarters, they need financial specialists, legal services, and all other kinds of management support like accounting, consulting, and training that cannot be produced in-house. Consequently, the new international division of labour leads to the clustering of advanced producer services in global cities that generate 'the capabilities for servicing, managing, and financing the global operations of firms and markets' (Sassen, 2001: 359; cf. Sassen, 1991, 2006a, 2006c, 2012). Global cities are therefore considered to be 'strategic sites for the management of the global economy and the production of the most advanced services and financial operations that have become key inputs for that work of managing global economic operations' (Sassen, 2006a: 32; cf. Sassen, 2012).

Although initially formulated for global cities, Sassen claims that the clustering argument is also valid for cities lower down the urban hierarchy, because '[p]arallel developments exist in cities that function as regional nodes – that is, at smaller geographical scales and lower levels of complexity than global cities' (Sassen, 2006a: 193; cf. Sassen, 2000: 139, 2006c: x, 2012: 323). This claim is probably responsible for the widely-held view in the global city debate that global cities like New York wear the future guise of cities lower down the urban hierarchy (e.g. Burgers, 1996; Mollenkopf, 2009; Mollenkopf & Castells, 1992; Vaattovaara & Kortteinen 2003). It is also often used to validate assessments of cities in the advanced economies *in general* according to the *global city* theoretical framework.

This might be too rigid an interpretation of that argument, however, and is problematic for two reasons. In the first place, right from the start, Sassen argued that the deindustrialization of archetypical industrial cities like Detroit does not lead to the clustering of advanced producer services in such cities, but in service-oriented urban economies like New York instead (Sassen-Koob, 1986: 88; Sassen, 1988: 23, 2001: 361, 2006a: 33, 2012: 324). Consequently, it is unlikely that the economic base of every city in the advanced economies will become similar to that of global cities. On the contrary, the examples of Detroit and New York imply that the economic bases of cities become less similar. Furthermore, some even argue that the clustering of advanced producer services in the most service-oriented cities not only feeds on the deindustrialization of former industrial strongholds, but also on the de-clustering of these services in other service-oriented cities (Hoyler, Kloosterman & Sokol, 2008; Sassen, 1995: 70, 2006a: 130-1, 2012: 8). In short, it is not at all clear whether the widely-held assumption in the global city debate that the economic base of cities will become similar to that of global cities is correct, as the global city theoretical framework makes the opposite claim. Chapter 2 will therefore first address the research question: *Does the economic base of cities in general increasingly resemble the economic base of global cities?*

Secondly, assuming that global cities wear the future guise of cities lower down the urban hierarchy is problematic, because international outsourcing, and the new international division of labour that stems from it, may indeed induce part of the clustering of advanced producer services that occurs in global cities. However, this does not mean that it drives this clustering in cities in the advanced economies in general. This assumption, just like the supposition that deindustrialization is the result of international outsourcing, is widely held to be true in the global city debate. Yet, the bulk of research findings on this matter suggests that both assumptions are invalid. If the impact of international outsourcing on urban labour markets in general is examined *according to the global city theoretical framework*, i.e. if it is assessed as the impact of deindustrialization and the clustering of advanced producer services, it will, consequently, be misinterpreted. Indeed, in that case, urban labour market changes induced by deindustrialization and the clustering of advanced producer services will be falsely attributed to international outsourcing and, consequently, on false grounds, to economic globalization. The second research question to be addressed in Chapter 2 is therefore: *Does international outsourcing drive deindustrialization and the clustering of advanced producer services in cities?*

1.2.2 Advanced producer services and labour demand

The basic claim in the global city theoretical framework concerning the impact of the clustering of advanced producer services on labour demand is laid down in the polarization thesis. This theory asserts that the clustering of advanced producer services in cities yields a high labour demand for both the highest and lowest occupational strata (Sassen-Koob, 1984b, 1986; Sassen, 1991, 2001, 2006a, 2012). The former are the professionals who work in the producer services, such as accountants, consultants, and financial specialists. The latter are the clerks, cleaners, and security workers who work in the producer services, employees in consumer services such as the hotel and catering industry, and service workers like nannies, housekeepers, and dog-walkers who cater to the lifestyles of the professionals employed in the advanced producer services (Sassen-Koob, 1984a, 1984b, 1985; Sassen, 1988, 2001, 2006a, 2012). Consequently, it might be anticipated that the occupational hierarchy will be most polarized in cities with the highest share of employment in the advanced producer services, and that the unemployment rate of less-educated urbanites will consequently be the lowest.

The polarization thesis is, however, disputed, as Chris Hamnett claimed that the clustering of advanced producer services leads to a professionalized, instead of a polarized, occupational hierarchy (1994a, 1994b, 1996a, 1996b, 2004; Hamnett & Cross, 1998). The crucial difference with the polarization thesis is that the professionalization theory asserts that this clustering leads to low instead of high labour demand for the lowest occupational stratum. What is important to emphasize here is that this is more than mere theoretical hair-splitting. This is because, according to the latter thesis, there will be a mismatch (i.e. high unemployment) between labour demand and supply at the bottom of the urban labour markets with the *highest* employment share in the advanced producer services. However, on the basis of polarization theory, it might be anticipated that there will be a mismatch at the bottom of urban labour markets in the cities with the *lowest* employment share in these advanced producer services.

Hamnett's critique provoked the polarization-versus-professionalization dispute that currently rages throughout the global city debate, and led to a substantial number of studies producing scattered results. As almost all these studies assess one city or a limited number of cities, and as some find polarization of the occupational hierarchy while others find professionalization, the precise impact of the clustering of advanced producer services on labour demand is still unclear. Various research findings even suggest that the occupational hierarchy in some cities will be polarized, while it will be professionalized in others, due to this clustering. Furthermore, the question of whether polarization and/or professionalization are indeed driven by the clustering of advanced producer services remains unanswered. Chapter 3 therefore concerns the following research question: *What is the impact of the clustering of advanced producer services on the unemployment rate of less-educated urbanites?*

After scrutinizing whether the impact of advanced producer services on unemployment rates is in accordance with the polarization or professionalization thesis, the resulting findings will be confronted with the theoretical notions in the debate on 'creative and bohemian' cities initiated by Richard Florida (2002, 2003, 2004, 2005; cf. Clark, 2003a, 2003b). In opposition to the productivist notions of professionalization and polarization in the global city debate, namely the theoretical notions based on the assumption that the organization of production is the primary driver of urban social life, Florida poses a consumerist alternative. His approach relates to the increasing importance of cultural industries, and the consumption of cultural activities, instead of the growing salience of advanced producer services. In Sassen's line of argument, the increasing prominence of cultural amenities and consumer services in cities is merely a derivative of the clustering of these advanced producer services, i.e. the 'consumption base' caters to the professionals employed in the 'production base'. Florida's argument, in contrast, postulates that advanced producer services settle in cities that are rich in cultural amenities, because these are the places where their potential employees prefer to live. If this is correct, the impact of the producer services on unemployment rates needs to be interpreted in a radically different way than is thus far the case in the global city debate; instead of resulting from the rearrangement of the global economy and the concomitant change in labour demand, the effect of these services is due to the lifestyle-driven residential preferences of the professionals working in the advanced producer services. Chapter 3 will therefore empirically scrutinize whether the clustering of these services, and the resulting unemployment rates of the less educated, need to be interpreted according to productivist arguments in the global city debate, Florida's consumerist claims, or both.

1.2.3 The new international division of labour and immigration

Immigration plays a vital role in the global city theoretical framework. In fact, the intellectual roots of this framework can be found in its arguments concerning the causes of immigration from newly-industrializing countries (Sassen-Koob, 1984b, 1985, 1986). In particular, it is asserted that the push factor of this immigration to cities in the advanced economies in general, and to global cities especially, is driven by so-called 'foreign direct investments'. These investments involve the outsourcing of parts of the production process to newly-industrializing countries in the form of production sites, which are often referred to as 'export processing zones'.

According to the global city theoretical framework, the 'disruption of traditional work structures' due to 'the transformation of subsistence workers into wage-labor' caused by foreign direct investments is what drives immigration from newly-industrializing countries to cities in the advanced economies (Sassen, 1988: 18; cf. Sassen-Koob, 1984b, 1985, 1986, Sassen, 2006b). It is claimed that due to the cultural links brought about by these investment flows between the sending and receiving countries, this migration often flows in the opposite direction, i.e. from the country invested in to the country from where these investments originate. It needs to be emphasized that this argument is not intended to replace classic migration theories that revolve around underdevelopment and population pressures. Instead, it is intended to be an additional theory with which to explain *new* migration flows. It argues that migration flows driven according to the logic of the classic migration theories are in the current phase of economic globalization accompanied by migration flows that are driven by foreign direct investments. As such, both theories can be valid, but for different types of migration flows. This has yet to be empirically substantiated, and the first research question addressed in Chapter 4 is therefore: *Can the new immigration to cities in the advanced economies be explained by foreign direct investments?*

The global city theoretical framework further argues that economic globalization is also a pull factor for immigration from newly-industrializing countries to cities in the advanced economies in general, and to global cities in particular. The theoretical rationale of this pull factor has been elaborated on in the previous section. The polarization thesis asserts that the clustering of advanced producer services brought about by the new international division of labour drives the demand for low-skilled service workers (Sassen-Koob, 1984a, 1984b, 1986; Sassen, 1988, 1991, 2001, 2006a). According to the global city theoretical framework, this labour demand is partly met by immigrants from newly-industrializing countries. This is a widely-held assumption in the global city debate, but, just like the push factor of immigration addressed above, it has not yet been systematically assessed. This might be problematic, as there are other theories, which do not revolve around the issue of labour demand, that can account for the settlement of immigrants in cities in the advanced economies, for instance, ideas concerning ethnic ties. The second research question to be addressed in Chapter 4 is therefore: *Does the clustering of advanced producer services attract immigrant labour from newly-industrializing countries?*

1.3 Scrutinizing the global city debate: blind spot

The sixth research question pertains to a blind spot in the global city theoretical framework concerning the impact of economic globalization on the social reality of cities. More specifically, this lacuna relates to the impact of immigration on urban labour markets. Such a blind spot does not come as a surprise because, in the global city theoretical framework, immigration is primarily considered to be a consequence, instead of a constitutive element, of economic globalization; as outlined above, it assumes that immigration is driven by foreign direct investment and the increased demand for low-skilled service workers that is the result. However, in the globalization literature at large, immigration is regarded as one of the constituting elements of economic globalization, i.e. the globalization of labour.

Several scholars have criticized the narrow focus of the global city theoretical framework on the clustering of advanced producer services as an indicator of the economic globalization of an urban economy (Benton-Short et al., 2005; Malecki & Ewers, 2007; Samers, 2002). Benton-Short et al. (2005) therefore call for researchers to 'expand the range of criteria used to assess the "globalness" of cities, to (...) include immigration in world city research and to call attention to cities experiencing dramatic social and demographic change due to immigration' (2005: 945). Their criticism, in short, boils down to both acknowledging that immigration is one of economic globalization's constituting forces and calling for it to be treated accordingly. Ironically, although the author of the global city theoretical framework also claims that '[i]mmigration is one of the constitutive processes of globalization today' (Sassen, 2006d: 315; cf. Sassen, 1998: xxi), it is not treated as such in her framework, and the impact of immigration on urban labour markets is consequently overlooked in the global city debate. As this debate aims to assess the impact of economic globalization on the economic and social reality of cities, this blind spot needs to be brought out into the open, and this study will do just that.

As well as assessing whether immigration from newly-industrializing countries is driven by 1) foreign direct investment and 2) the demand by services for low-skilled labour, this study will also assess the impact of immigration on urban labour markets on the basis of substitution theory.

This thesis applies classic economic logic to the market for labour in which immigrants are considered to be substitutes for natives and former waves of immigrants (Chiswick, 1982; Johnson, 1980). As most immigrants in the advanced economies come from less-developed countries and are low-skilled, this substitution manifests itself at the bottom of urban labour markets. Consequently, on the basis of the substitution thesis, immigration, i.e. a supply shock in labour, leads to a downward pressure on the wages of less-educated urbanites and, ultimately, to their unemployment.

Looked at in this way, the question of whether immigration leads to labour market substitution is a crucial one for the central aim of this study. Indeed, if migration flows to cities in the advanced economies do not lead to labour market substitution, this would suggest that the current phase of economic globalization calls for a new conceptual framework to understand its impact on cities, as Sassen does indeed claim. It would certainly suggest that the global city theoretical framework allows us to better understand the impact of the current phase of economic globalization on urban labour markets than the old concepts (in this case, substitution) that social scientists have tended to use to study cities. Indeed, this is the very reason why Sassen formulated her framework in the first place, as her quote at the start of this introductory chapter reveals (cf. Sassen, 2012: ix). And according to this framework, migration flows to cities in the advanced economies are supposed to be absorbed by a high demand for low-skilled labour in the service industries. As a result, the productivist logic of the global city theoretical framework simply does not allow labour market substitution due to immigration to exist.

However, as argued above, the question of whether the clustering of advanced producer services leads to polarization (i.e. a high labour demand for less-educated urbanites) is still an empirical one (research question 3). The same applies to the question of whether the settlement of immigrants in cities is completely determined by labour market logic (research questions 4 and 5). As a consequence, the issue of whether or not immigration leads to labour market substitution is also empirical. Looked at in this way, the rejection of substitution theory would be a vital step in confirming the empirical validity of crucial arguments in the global city theoretical framework on labour demand in, and immigration to, cities in the advanced economies. On the other hand, its corroboration would suggest that these arguments are in need of some adjustment. The validity of the substitution thesis for contemporary cities will therefore be assessed on the basis of research question 6: *What is the impact of immigration on unemployment among less-educated urbanites?*

1.4 Research questions

Table 1.1 Research questions by chapter

	Research questions	Chapter
1	Does the economic base of cities in general increasingly resemble the economic base of global cities?	2
2	Does international outsourcing drive deindustrialization and the clustering of advanced producer services in cities?	2
3	What is the impact of the clustering of advanced producer services on the unemployment rate of less-educated urbanites?	3
4	Can the new immigration to cities in the advanced economies be explained by foreign direct investments?	4
5	Does the clustering of advanced producer services attract immigrant labour from newly-industrializing countries?	4
6	What is the impact of immigration on unemployment among less-educated urbanites?	5

1.5 Research framework

To answer the research questions outlined above, there is a need for a comparative framework that satisfies two conditions: 1) comparable cities in a 2) globalized economy, as conceptualized in the global city theoretical framework. Starting with the latter condition, the cities to be compared need to be situated in a country with substantial outward foreign investment flows, and must include one global city that allegedly functions as the cockpit for the globally-dispersed production processes stemming from these investments. Put differently, there is a need to compare cities in a country that: hosts a substantial number of international headquarters of firms with a globally-dispersed production process; and (according to the global city theoretical framework) consequently has a global city that produces the capabilities that enable those firms to coordinate and control that process.

The comparative framework called for as a way to answer the research questions set out above also needs to compare a substantial number of cities in an advanced economy, while controlling for state-led intervention in the labour market. As these interventions are responsible for differences across urban labour markets, failing to control for them will make it very difficult to uncover the extent to which the findings can really be attributed to the clustering of advanced producer services, immigration, or a combination thereof, as argued in the global city theoretical framework and global city debate, in the chapters that follow (cf. Burgers & Musterd, 2002; Vaattovaara & Kortteinen, 2003; Van der Waal, 2010).

The first step of the case selection involves finding out which advanced economies stand out as being the most globalized according to the central theoretical notions in the global city debate. To do this, I measured the openness of advanced economies by assessing the extent of their investments abroad as a share of their gross domestic product. This indicates the extent to which the firms in these countries have a globally-dispersed production process. Table 1.2 ranks advanced economies according to their investments abroad for each year in the period 1995 to 2010, which is the time span that can be scrutinized by means of the data in the empirical chapters that follow. The table indicates that there is some variation in the countries that belong to the ten most open economies during the assessed time span. As a consequence, Table 1.3 ranks the most open advanced economies measured according to the number of years that they have belonged to the ten most open economies within the assessed period. This step reveals that Belgium, the Netherlands, and Switzerland are the most open economies with respect to investments abroad.[1]

Unsurprisingly, all three of these countries contain a global city according to the parameters of the global city theoretical framework. Indeed, despite the conceptual confusion over what the global city concept precisely means, and how this relates to the world city concepts of Friedmann (1986; cf. Friedmann & Wolff, 1982) and Braudel (1984), what is undisputed is the most important feature of such cities for the research at hand (Taylor, 2004): the clustering of globally-interconnected advanced producer services (Sassen, 2001, 2006a; cf. Taylor, 2004). The idea behind this clustering is that due to the new international division of labour, there is a need for the production of control capacity for the management of globally-dispersed production chains. Advanced producer services produce these 'capabilities for servicing, managing, and financing the global operations of firms and markets' (Sassen, 2001: 359). To do this, these services 'need to provide a global service which [means] a global network of affiliates or some other form of partnership' (Sassen, 2001: xxi). The clustering of these services is thus the central element in the global city theoretical framework, and the pivot upon which everything hinges when it comes to its arguments concerning the labour market changes about to be assessed.

1 Note that Belgium and Luxemburg were combined in the UNCTAD statistics until 2002.

Table 1.2 Rank order of outward FDI of advanced economies, as measured by their investments abroad as a share of their gross domestic product (1995-2010)

Rank	1995	1996	1997	1998	1999	2000	2001	2002	2003	2004	2005	2006	2007	2008	2009	2010
1	NL	NL	CH	FI	BE	BE	BE	LU	BE	LU	IC	IC	LU	BE	IC	LU
2	SE	CH	NL	BE	NL	FI	NL	IE	MA	IC	LU	CH	IC	LU	IE	CH
3	BE	NO	SE	SE	UK	NL	DK	NL	NL	IE	NL	LU	BE	CY	EE	IE
4	UK	BE	UK	NL	CH	CH	CH	FI	SE	BE	CH	BE	UK	CH	SE	BE
5	CH	FI	FI	UK	DK	DK	FI	CY	CH	CH	BE	BM	CH	NL	CH	NL
6	NZ	UK	CA	CH	FR	SE	FR	BE	CY	SE	NO	IL	AT	IE	NO	NO
7	CA	CA	NO	CA	SE	UK	ES	ES	PR	NL	SE	NL	ES	AT	NL	SE
8	NO	DE	BE	IE	ES	FR	PR	SE	UK	ES	IE	ES	SE	UK	FR	FI
9	DK	MA	EE	DE	IE	ES	CA	CA	IE	CY	DK	IE	IE	SE	CA	IL
10	DE	FR	ES	ES	DE	PR	IC	IC	IC	CA	FR	SE	EE	FR	LU	DE

Source: UNCTAD

Legend: AT = Austria, BE = Belgium, BM = Bermuda, CA = Canada, CH = Switzerland, CY = Cyprus, DE = Germany, DK = Denmark, EE = Estonia, ES = Spain, FI = Finland, FR = France, IE = Ireland, IC = Iceland, IL = Israel, LU = Luxemburg, MA = Malta, NL = Netherlands, NO = Norway, NZ = New Zealand, SE = Sweden, UK = United Kingdom

Table 1.3 Number of times that a country belongs to the ten most open advanced economies, if measured as their investments abroad as a share of their gross domestic product (1995-2010)

Rank	Country	Times
1	Belgium	15
	Netherlands	15
	Switzerland	15
4	Sweden	14
5	Ireland	11
6	Canada	9
	Spain	9
	United Kingdom	9
9	Iceland	8
	Luxemburg	8

Source: UNCTAD

In accordance with this line of argument, Belgium, Switzerland, and the Netherlands play host to cities – Brussels, Zurich, and Amsterdam, respectively – that score very high on the indicators mentioned above for determining whether a city is a global city. All three of these global cities rank high on these indicators, although Amsterdam always outranks the other two (Sassen, 1991, 1994, 2000, 2001, 2006a, 2006d, 2007, 2012). Indeed, in Sassen's most recent studies on this matter, Amsterdam often belongs to the ten most globalized cities. Brussels and Zurich, on the other hand, almost never do (Sassen, 2012). Moreover, various other studies report similar findings (Alderson & Beckfield, 2004; Beaverstock et al., 1999; Derudder et al., 2003; Derudder & Taylor, 2005; Neal, 2008; Taylor, 2002, 2004; Taylor & Aranya, 2008). In these studies, which without exception find that New York and London are the most globally-interconnected cities, as Sassen claims, Amsterdam also scores very high; almost without exception, it is one of the top ten most globally-connected cities. Again, in all these studies, Brussels and Zurich score far lower than Amsterdam. Nevertheless, just being ranked lower on indicators of global city functions does not rule out the host countries of Brussels and Zurich as strategic cases for testing the hypotheses needed to answer the six research questions in this study. However, the scores of the two cities on the other necessary condition for such an assessment do have this effect.

As well as being embedded in an open economy and located in a country that plays host to a global city, the cities to be compared need to be assessed while controlling for state-led labour market intervention. In this respect, the Netherlands differs greatly from Belgium and Switzerland in that it had a highly centralized welfare state in the time span being assessed, whereas the other two countries are more or less the polar opposite on this matter (cf. Burgers & Musterd, 2001; Musterd, Ostendorf & Breebaart, 1998; Newman & Thornley, 1996; Parkinson et al., 1988). Indeed, these two countries have the two most challenging government structures that a researcher aiming to compare cities can face: Belgium has a federation of three government regions, Flanders, Wallonia, and Brussels, while Switzerland has a federation of cantons, each with its own constitution, legislature, and government. Consequently, assessing the impact of economic globalization on the social and economic reality of cities by way of systematic city comparisons would be very challenging. In contrast, the substantial number of cities embedded within the centralized welfare state of the Netherlands is very suitable for rigorously testing the arguments in the global city theoretical framework and debate.

In short, the Netherlands is the most strategic case for assessing the empirical validity of the theoretical notions in the global city theoretical framework and global city debate. This is because it is an advanced economy that combines 1) a high degree of economic openness with 2) a substantial number of cities, including the global city of Amsterdam, in a highly-centralized institutional setting. It does, however, share one shortcoming with all the other countries in the world when it comes to answering the research questions at hand: the relevant, available data relate, without exception, to the state instead of the urban level. Consequently, considerable efforts were made to construct city-level datasets out of state-level data (see Appendix B for a detailed description of all the datasets used in this study and the operationalization of all the variables). This is, of course, a necessary condition for answering the research questions, but it should be emphasized that it did have some limitations, which will be addressed each time they occur in the analyses that follow.

Statistics Netherlands (*CBS*) discerns 22 metropolitan areas in the Netherlands (for reasons of brevity, they will often simply be referred to as 'cities' in the chapters that follow) about which most of the necessary data could be retrieved for the period 1995-2008. Some analyses are, however, made on a smaller range of years due to data limitations. As a consequence, the period addressed in most of the analyses in this book roughly ranges from the mid-1990s up to the financial crisis that started in 2008.

2 The changing economic base of cities

The geographical dispersal of economic activities that marks globalization (...) is a key factor feeding the growth and importance of central corporate functions (...), that is the work of managing, coordinating, servicing, financing a firm's network of operations. [These] become so complex that increasingly the headquarters of large global firms outsource them [to] highly specialized service firms: accounting, legal, public relations (...) and other such services [which] are subject to agglomeration economies (Sassen, 2001: xix-xx).

2.1 Introduction

The aim of this chapter is to assess the central claims in the global city debate concerning the impact of the new international division of labour on the economic base of cities in the advanced economies. According to the global city theoretical framework, this division of labour manifests itself as a combination of deindustrialization and the clustering of advanced producer services in global cities. This does not in any way imply that the economic base of all cities in the advanced economies becomes roughly identical to that of global cities. Nevertheless, this assumption clearly underlies the standard research practice in the global city debate, in which the impact of the new international division of labour on urban labour markets *in general* is interpreted on the basis of the global city theoretical framework. Such practice comes down to assuming that the economic base of global cities reveals the future guise of cities lower down the urban hierarchy (e.g. Burgers, 1996; Mollenkopf, 2009; Mollenkopf & Castells, 1992; Vaattovaara & Kortteinen, 2003).

This might be problematic for at least two reasons. In the first place, the global city theoretical framework asserts two other scenarios. That industrial employment declined in all cities in the advanced economies is undisputed. However, when it comes to the essential aspect of global city formation – the clustering of advanced producer services – the global city theoretical framework makes a clear distinction between global or service-oriented cities in general on the one hand, and former industrial strongholds on the other. The framework claims that the growth in employment in the advanced producer services in the former type of city is much stronger than in the latter. Consequently, it might be expected that the economic base of these two types of city will become less, instead of more, similar. Furthermore, some claim that the clustering of advanced producer services in some service-oriented cities feeds on the de-clustering of these services in other such cities. After addressing the scenarios on the clustering of advanced producer services in Section 2.2, and assessing their empirical validity in the section that follows, the first research question to be answered in the concluding section is: *Does the economic base of cities in general increasingly resemble the economic base of global cities?*

Assuming that the economic base of global cities reveals the future guise of cities lower down the urban hierarchy is, in the second place, problematic because, especially for cities lower down the urban hierarchy than global cities, there is room for doubt as to whether deindustrialization and the clustering of advanced producer services can be attributed to the new international division of labour brought about by outsourcing parts of the production process to newly-industrializing countries. As a result of this assumption in the global city debate, the standard research practice boils down to mapping the consequences of deindustrialization and the clustering of advanced producer services, and subsequently attributing them to the new international division of labour. What this means for many research findings in the global city debate is dealt with in Section 2.4, while Section 2.5 answers the second research question: *Does international outsourcing drive deindustrialization and the clustering of advanced producer services in cities?*

2.2 Three scenarios on employment growth in the advanced producer services

2.2.1 The two clustering arguments in the global city theoretical framework

The global city theoretical framework asserts that due to the new international division of labour, very little manufacturing remains in the advanced economies, as it is outsourced to newly-industrializing countries. Coordinating and controlling the globally-dispersed production process that stems from this international division of labour is a highly complex endeavour. This is particularly the case when comparisons are made to the task faced by the classic vertically-integrated firms that are characteristic of the industrial era, which is often referred to as the Fordist era. As the coordination and control capacities needed for a globally-dispersed production process are too complex to produce in-house, this production is outsourced to advanced producer services. Consequently, the new international division of labour leads to the clustering of advanced producer services in global cities that produce 'the capabilities for servicing, managing, and financing the global operations of firms and markets' (Sassen, 2001: 359; cf. Sassen, 1991, 2006a, 2006c, 2012). Put differently, 'the growth of these sectors (...) is associated with the globalization of economic activity and the new organizational structures that such globalization engenders' (Sassen-Koob, 1986: 86).

Initially, this clustering argument was formulated for just three cities, as the subtitle of the first edition of *The Global City. New York, London, Tokyo* reveals (1991). Recently, however, Sassen has claimed that there are now 'about seventy' global cities (Sassen, 2012: 7). This does not mean, though, that the clustering argument is only formulated for this limited number of global cities. Indeed, it is argued that the clustering of advanced producer services will also occur in cities lower down the urban hierarchy: '[p]arallel developments exist in cities that function as regional nodes – that is, at smaller geographical scales and lower levels of complexity than global cities' (Sassen, 2006a: 193; cf. Friedmann, 1995: 22; Sassen, 2000: 139; 2006c: x, 2012: 323). Yet, this does not imply that the economic base of *all* cities in the advanced economies becomes identical to that of global cities. According to Sassen, the concentration of advanced producer services in the most service-oriented urban economies is a 'predatory process', in that it feeds on the industrial decline in former industrial strongholds (Sassen, 1998: xxv, 2001: 7-8, 2006a: 130, 2007: 112, 2012: 8).

The central argument in the clustering debate is that due to the new international division of labour, former industrial strongholds see employment in manufacturing industries decline, as it is outsourced to newly-industrializing countries, while global cities see employment in advanced producer services grow *because* this outsourcing needs the coordination of the services located there. Moreover, a similar, predatory process will manifest itself in an attenuated form in service-oriented cities that function as 'regional nodes', that is, cities that function as global cities only on the smaller geographical (read: national or regional) scale (Sassen, 2006a: 193; cf. Friedmann, 1995: 22; Sassen, 2000: 139, 2006c: x, 2012: 323). According to this line of reasoning, these regional nodes will also see their share of employment in the advanced producer services increase more markedly than in the former industrial strongholds. In short, according to the global city theoretical framework, employment in the advanced producer services experiences stronger growth in global and service-oriented cities that function as regional nodes than in former industrial strongholds. This is because the clustering of advanced producer services in the former feeds on the deindustrialization of the latter.

The primary example of this scenario is the economic fortunes of Detroit vis-à-vis New York in recent decades. According to Sassen, 'the manufacturing jobs that Detroit began to lose in the 1970s and 1980s fed a growing demand for specialised corporate services in New York City to coordinate and manage a now globally distributed auto manufacturing system' (2006a: 71; cf. Sassen-Koob, 1986: 88; Sassen, 1988: 23, 2001: 361, 2006a: 33, 2012: 34). Others have made similar arguments, not specifically for global cities, but for service-oriented cities in general. Kasarda (1985; cf. Kasarda & Friedrichs, 1985, 1986), for example, stressed that the growth in the advanced producer services in former industrial strongholds in the US, as well as in West Germany, already lagged behind this clustering in service-oriented cities in the early 1980s (cf. Scott & Storper, 1986). On the basis of similar findings, Dangschat (1994) roughly discerned 'winners' and 'losers' in the transition to a post-industrial economy. In his dichotomy, the 'winners' are cities that already had a substantial share of producer services in their economy before deindustrialization kicked in during the 1970s; New York, London, Frankfurt, and Amsterdam, for instance. The 'losers', on the other hand, are cities that depended greatly on manufacturing industries in the 1970s, such as Liverpool, cities in the German Ruhr area, Rotterdam, and the so-called 'Rust Belt cities' in the US like Detroit (cf. Cheshire, 1990; Knapp & Schmitt, 2008; Meijer, 1993; Sassen, 2006a: 71, 2012: 34).

Sassen's arguments on global cities and regional nodes (Sassen-Koob, 1986: 8; Sassen, 1988: 23, 2001: 361, 2006: 33), and those of Kasarda (1985; Kasarda & Friedrichs, 1985, 1986) and Dangschat (1994) on service-oriented cities in general, all boil down to the expectation that, just like the advanced economies in general, all cities in the advanced economies deindustrialized and experienced employment growth in the advanced producer services. Yet, according to these authors, the growth in the advanced producer services in service-oriented cities, especially global cities, is much stronger than in former industrial strongholds. Accordingly, this is what will, from now on, be referred to as the first scenario.

Some findings on the clustering of advanced producer services in cities even point in the direction of a double predatory process (Scenario 2). Indeed, it was found that the clustering of advanced producer services in some service-oriented urban economies not only feeds on the deindustrialization of former industrial strongholds, as argued in the global city theoretical framework (Scenario 1), but also on the de-clustering of advanced producer services in other service-oriented cities within the same country (Scenario 2) (cf. Hoyler, Kloosterman & Sokol, 2008; Sassen, 1995: 70, 2006a: 130-1, 2012: 8). This is a process that has been documented in Australia for Sydney at the cost of Melbourne (Daly & Stimson, 1992), in Switzerland for Zurich at the cost of Basel (Keil & Ronneberger, 1992), in Canada for Toronto at the cost of Montreal (Levine, 1990), and in Frankfurt at the cost of six other German financial centres (Sassen, 2012: 8).

The reasoning behind this double predatory thesis reflects the clustering argument in the global city theoretical framework, i.e. geographical proximity to important clients –multinationals' headquarters – and the added value due to the (informal) exchange of knowledge and information between professionals in the advanced producer services (cf. Storper & Venables, 2004). If this also happens in the Netherlands, not all service-oriented Dutch cities will see their share of the advanced producer services rise much more than that of the former industrial strongholds, as argued in the global city theoretical framework (Scenario 1). This is because some of these service-oriented cities will see this share increase at the cost of other such places. Despite this difference between the predatory (Scenario 1) and the double predatory theses (Scenario 2), they share the central expectation that *Dutch cities diverge in their share of employment in the advanced producer services.* If this is correct, many cities, most notably former industrial strongholds, will become less similar to the global city of Amsterdam when it comes to their employment share in the advanced producer services.

2.2.2 The clustering argument in the global city debate

As stated above, it is often assumed in the global city debate that the economic base of all cities becomes similar to that of global cities (Scenario 3). This assumption underlies the standard research practice of interpreting the impact of economic globalization in all cities in the advanced economies on the basis of either the polarization and professionalization theses (see Table A1 in Appendix A for a detailed list of these studies), or other arguments in the global city theoretical framework (e.g. Amen et al., 2006; Brenner & Keil, 2006). This line of reasoning can be found from the early days of the global city debate onwards. It started with Mollenkopf and Castells (1992), who, in the often cited volume *Dual City: Restructuring New York,* aimed to 'illuminate how global economic restructuring influenced the weaving of the social, cultural, and political fabric in (...) New York' (1992: 5-6). These authors claimed that '[t]he New York experience (...) can be viewed as central to understanding late twentieth century post-industrial transformation' (5). This comment inspired Vaattovaara and Kortteinen, among many others in the global city debate, to apply the polarization and professionalization theses to the Helsinki region, and their reasoning was based on the following argument: '[T]he global city-thesis claims that the developments in global cities are paradigmatic for those in other cities (...) In other words, what is already manifest and obvious in the global cities is about to become the trend for cities at the lower levels of the global urban hierarchy' (2003: 2128).

This argument can of course still be interpreted as being in line with the global city theoretical framework, as it is not clear whether it asserts that *all* cities lower down the urban hierarchy are catching up with global cities or merely the most service-oriented cities. Yet recently Mollenkopf, again, claimed that 'the economic functions that are concentrated in global cities – that some scholars think distinguish them from other, lesser cities – are growing relatively faster outside the big central cities and in metropolitan areas lower down the national and international hierarchy (...) leaving even declining industrial cities different kind of places than they were in the past' (2009: 273). Although this argument is neither made with reference to empirical studies, nor based on a line of argument as to why cities lower down the urban hierarchy are catching up with global cities, Mollenkopf seems quite convinced that this is actually happening. The central expectation of this third scenario, then, is that *the employment share in the advanced producer services did rise in all Dutch cities, but more so in cities that previously lagged behind in this respect.* If this is correct, all Dutch cities will become more similar to the global city of Amsterdam when it comes to their employment share in the advanced producer services.

2.3 Assessing employment growth in the advanced producer services

This section will examine the changing economic base of cities, and includes an assessment of the trends in the clustering of advanced producer services in the 22 metropolitan areas in the Netherlands between 1995 and 2008 (see Appendix B for the data used, the operationalization of the variables, and a map with the delineation of these metropolitan areas). This will provide an answer to the question of whether the economic base of these cities has become more similar to that of global cities in this period, as often argued in the global city debate (Scenario 3), or less similar, as asserted in the global city theoretical framework (Scenarios 1 and 2).

I have calculated the employment shares in manufacturing for the years 1995 to 2007 for each city (see Appendix C). As the trends in employment shares in manufacturing are downwards for each city, and because there is no theoretical argument to expect that this would be otherwise, this finding will no longer be discussed. Instead, from now on I will focus on the trends in the employment shares that are the subject of debate, i.e. those in the advanced producer services. I first calculated these employment shares for each city for each year in the period 1995-2007. Subsequently, I calculated the mean score for the 22 metropolitan areas combined for each of those years. The trend line of the triangles in Figure 2.1 indicates the results of these calculations. At first sight, it is clear that the mean share of producer services did rise in the period assessed. The trend did, however, experience a relapse between 2000 and 2004, probably as a consequence of the downward economic trend in the Netherlands after the economic boom of the 1990s. Nevertheless, the overall trend for the 22 Dutch metropolitan areas between 1995 and 2008 is very clear, and not particularly surprising, the share of advanced producer services did grow.

Figure 2.1 Trends in the means and standard deviations of the employment shares in the advanced producer services in the 22 Dutch metropolitan areas

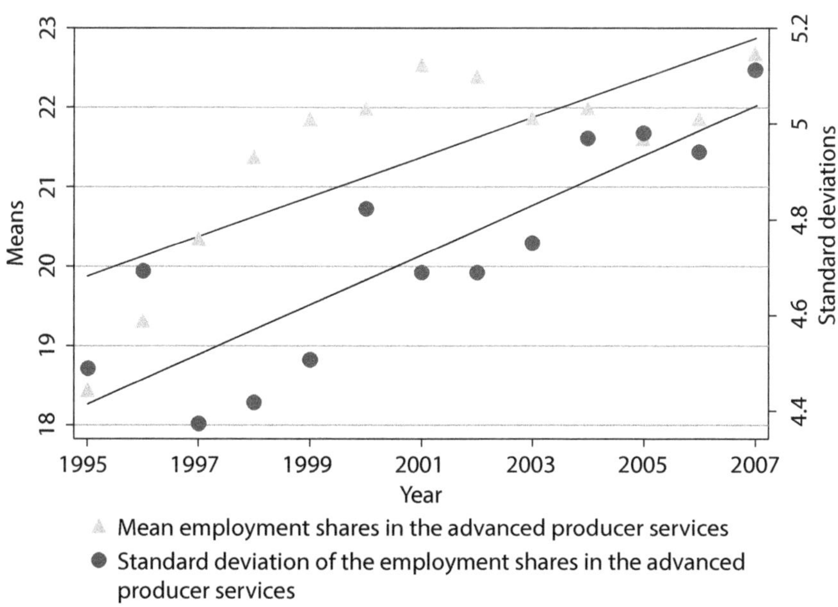

However, this does not mean that the economic base of Dutch cities increasingly resembles that of the global city of Amsterdam. The trend line of the standard deviations in the employment shares of the producer services (the one based on the dots in Figure 2.1) indicates that the economic base of Dutch cities diverged instead of converged. The standard deviation measures the distribution around the mean score (a higher standard deviation indicates a wider distribution), and Figure 2.1 clearly shows that the deviation of the employment shares in the advanced producer services increased in a strongly linear fashion. This means that between 1995 and 2008, the employment shares in the advanced producer services in the 22 metropolitan areas under scrutiny *diverged*: in some cities this share increased more sharply than in others.

The diverging trends in the employment shares of the advanced producer services seen in Figure 2.1 reveal that the economic base of Dutch cities did *not* become more similar, as expected on the basis of the predatory and double predatory theses formulated by Sassen (1998: xxv, 2001: 7-8, 2006a: 130, 2007: 112, 2012: 8) in the global city theoretical framework. As a consequence, this is contrary to what is often expected in the global city debate (e.g. Mollenkopf, 2009; Vaattovaara & Kortteinen, 2003). Assessing the trends for each city separately will demonstrate precisely what is occurring, as there are at least two scenarios that can account for this divergence trends. The first of these is that employment in the advanced producer services did rise in all metropolitan areas, but most strongly in the most service-oriented cities (the predatory thesis/Scenario 1). The second scenario differs from the first in that this stronger growth only occurs in some service-oriented cities, as other such locations actually see their share of employment in the advanced producer services decline (double predatory thesis/Scenario 2). The trends depicted in Figures 2.2, 2.3, and 2.4 can shed some light on this matter.

Figure 2.2 demonstrates the trends in employment in the advanced producer services in the seven most service-oriented cities, as measured by their employment share in those services in 1995. Meanwhile, Figure 2.3 highlights these trends for the seven most manufacturing-oriented cities under scrutiny, as measured by their employment share in manufacturing, also in 1995. Figure 2.4 demonstrates the trend line of the *difference* in the average employment shares in the advanced producer services between those two categories of cities. This clearly indicates that the difference increased in the assessed period, which would be expected on the basis of the predatory thesis. In other words, in the most service-oriented cities, the employment share in the advanced producer services increased much more than in former industrial strongholds. Yet, underlying these trends in average employment shares, the trend lines of individual cities suggest that the scenario labelled as double predatory growth is also occurring in the Netherlands. What stands out most in Figure 2.2 is that the Dutch city that was most service-oriented in 1995 – Arnhem – endured a decline in employment in the advanced producer services, while Amsterdam, Utrecht, and Amersfoort experienced substantial increases in the same period. This suggests that the growth in the latter three cities occurred at the cost of growth in the former. Moreover, in line with the double predatory thesis, the rise in employment in the advanced producer services is most prominent in the global city of Amsterdam. In summary, Figures 2.1 to 2.4 demonstrate that the economic base of cities is diverging in the Netherlands, and thus not converging to the global city model. Furthermore, the trend lines in these figures suggest that the reason for this divergence is twofold: 1) the predatory growth of advanced producer services in service-oriented cities at the cost of the growth of those services in former industrial strongholds (predatory thesis); and 2) the predatory growth of these services in the global city of Amsterdam at the cost of advanced producer services growth in cities that were already very service-oriented, like Arnhem.

Figure 2.2 Trends in the employment shares in the advanced producer services in the seven most service-oriented Dutch cities

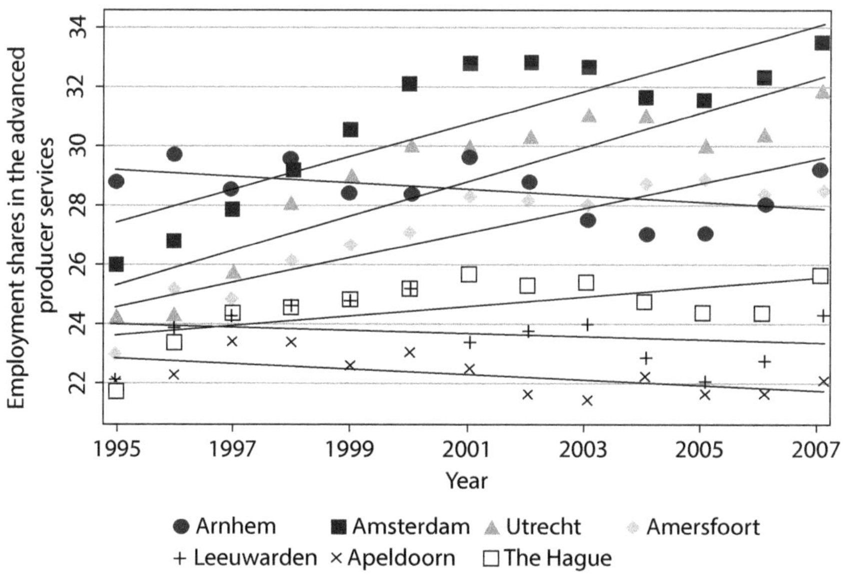

Figure 2.3 Trends in the employment shares in the advanced producer services in the seven most manufacturing-oriented Dutch cities

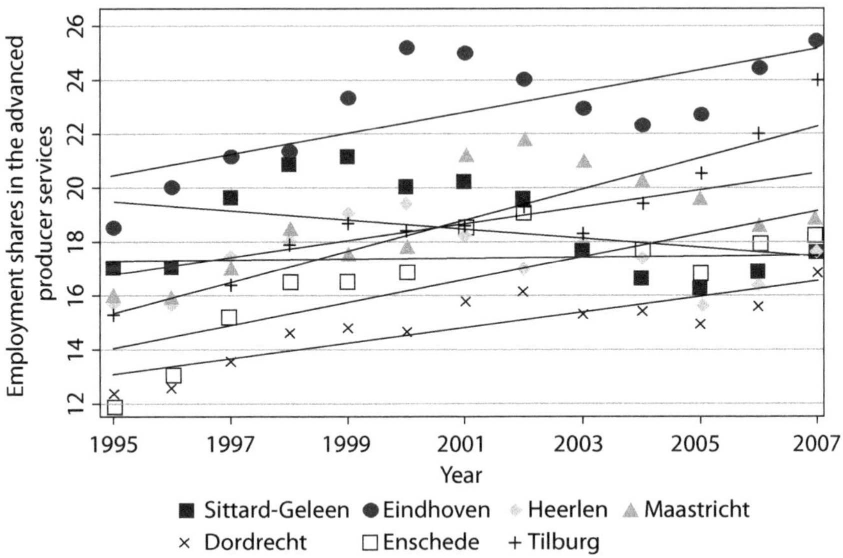

The economic base of Dutch cities did not, then, become more similar, but instead diverged between 1995 and 2008. The question that remains in this chapter is: to what extent can this be attributed to the new international division of labour, as argued in both the global city theoretical framework and the global city debate?

2.4 What drives deindustrialization and growth in services?

The previous section assessed the clustering of advanced producer services in Dutch cities between 1995 and 2008, which was accompanied by strong deindustrialization. According to the global city theoretical framework, these two processes are interconnected and related to the new international division of labour (Sassen, 1991, 2001, 2006a, 2012), and the bulk of studies in the global city debate simply reproduce this argument. In the latest – global – phase of capitalism, capital has managed, so it is argued, to disperse its production process on a global scale, so that it can extract more surplus value from labour than in the preceding Fordist/industrial phase of capitalist production.

Figure 2.4 Trend in the difference between the average employment shares in the advanced producer services in the seven most service-oriented Dutch cities and the average employment shares in the advanced producer services in the seven most manufacturing-oriented Dutch cities

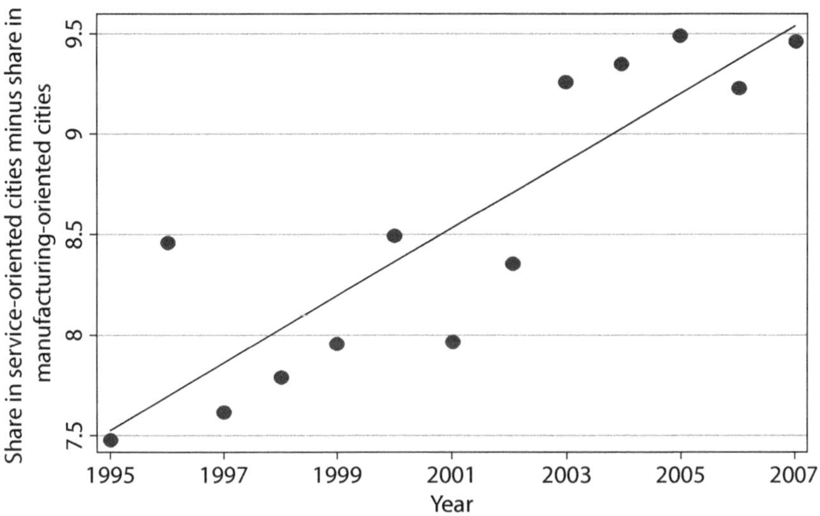

In the Fordist/industrial phase, production took place in vertically integrated firms in the advanced economies. One of the consequences of this type of production is that the price of labour in these countries increased substantially after World War II. As low-skilled labour is more abundant in newly-industrializing countries, the price of labour is much lower than in the advanced economies. By outsourcing parts of the production process to these countries, capital can therefore extract more surplus value from labour than in the advanced economies, where the price of low-skilled labour is high. According to the global city theoretical framework, this is what has actually happened in recent decades, and is what drives the fall in employment in manufacturing in the advanced economies (see Appendix C on the deindustrialization of Dutch cities). At face value, this theoretical rationale seems plausible, which is probably why this 'outsourcing-deindustrialization nexus' is very prominent in public and political debates in Europe and the United States (including, of course, for reasons of political opportunism; cf. Doogan, 2009). Every plant closure in the advanced economies is accompanied by gloomy reports on the economic future of European and American workers in an age when companies, with the help of information and communication technology and the deregulation of global markets, can outsource their production process to wherever it yields the highest profits.

In the academic debates, on the other hand, there are more theories to explain why deindustrialization did occur in the advanced economies, and outsourcing is not even the most prominent of these explanations. In fact, more than two decades of empirical research on this matter shows that international outsourcing is only responsible for a small part of the deindustrialization of Europe and the United states. In 2007, an OECD study by Molnar, Pain, and Taglioni reviewed the bulk of the empirical research conducted on the impact of investment from multinationals in newly-industrializing countries. They concluded that 'some studies have found evidence of substitution between employment in foreign affiliates and parent companies, but others have found that the two are complements. In either case the reported effects are generally small and may vary over time' (2007: 33). Similar arguments can be found in two additional studies on the same topic. Hijzen and Swaim conclude:

> Offshoring has no effect or a slight positive effect on sectoral employment. Offshoring within the same industry (intra-industry offshoring) reduces the labour-intensity of production, but does not affect overall industry employment. Inter-industry offshoring does not affect labour-intensity, but may have a positive effect on overall industry employment. These findings suggest that the productivity gains from offshoring are sufficiently large that the jobs created by higher sales completely offset the jobs lost by relocating certain production stages to foreign production sites. (2007: 86)

Furthermore, the main finding of the chapter in the *OECD Employment Outlook* of 2007, entitled *OECD Workers in the Global Economy: Increasingly Vulnerable?,* is also very clear on this matter: 'offshoring has no effect or a positive effect on sectoral employment' (2007: 3; cf. Brady et al., 2007; Crinò, 2009: 233-4; see however: Zapkau & Schwens, 2014).[2]

2 In the globalization literature, the terms outsourcing and offshoring are often used as synonyms. However, strictly speaking, these are labels for different processes. The former concerns the purchase of goods and services produced abroad that were previously produced by firms themselves (i.e. in-house). Offshoring concerns a similar practice, except that these goods and services are produced *by the same company that purchases them, only in a foreign establishment* (Molnar et al., 2007). However, in the debate on what drives the deindustrialization of the advanced economies, both processes boil down to the same logic: if they did not exist, these goods and services would need to be produced in the home country of the company that purchases them.

In short, the bulk of the available evidence suggests that the deindustrialization of Europe and the United States cannot, or at most can very minimally, be attributed to the practice of multinationals relocating part of their production process abroad. This finding begs the question as to how this deindustrialization came about in recent decades, and how it is possible that the share of employment in manufacturing declined strongly in the advanced economies. Several studies have addressed this question in what has become known as the 'technology-versus-trade debate' (cf. Krugman, 1994, 1996). According to the technology argument, manufacturing did not decline in the advanced economies as a result of outsourcing to, or imports from, newly-industrializing countries, as Faux (2006), Saeger (1997), and Wood (1994), for instance, argue; instead, this was due to productivity growth owing to the automation of the production process (Kollmeyer, 2009; Krugman & Lawrence, 1993; Rowthorn & Ramaswamy, 1997, 1999; see however: Onaran, 2012).

Others stress that, along with productivity growth in manufacturing, two other factors account for deindustrialization and the declining share of employment in manufacturing compared to the position in commercial services in Europe and the US. The first of these factors concerns the shift in national demand from manufactured goods to services, while the second relates to the commodification of the household economy – child care, care of the elderly, housekeeping, and the like – due to the increasing labour market participation of women (Esping-Andersen, 1999; Iversen & Cusack, 2000; Kollmeyer, 2009; Rowthorn & Ramaswamy, 1999; see however: Alderson, 1999). Unlike manufacturing, these kinds of services are very labour-intensive, as they often require human contact and are therefore difficult to automate.

In short, higher productivity growth in manufacturing than in services, changing national demand, and commodification of the household economy largely made the advanced economies post-industrial by the turn of the millennium, while the outsourcing of parts of the production process to newly-industrializing countries rarely did so. Accordingly, the consequences of deindustrialization for labour demand should not be attributed to international outsourcing, as is the standard argument in the global city debate. To be clear, the question as to whether processes of economic globalization other than outsourcing are responsible for the deindustrialization of cities in the advanced economies is an open one that goes far beyond the scope of this study. It is, for example, more than likely that global economic competition is an important driver of the technological innovation that drives deindustrialization. Yet, what is important here is that the argument in the global city theoretical framework concerning deindustrialization, which revolves around international outsourcing, seems to have no empirical basis.

The same logic can be applied to the rising share of commercial services in cities in the advanced economies in general. The growing share of employment in these services has no clear link with outsourcing, contrary to what is assumed in the global city debate. Unlike the bulk of commercial services in cities in the advanced economies, the aspect of the advanced producer services in *global cities* that produces 'the capabilities for servicing, managing, and financing the global operations of firms and markets' (Sassen, 2001: 359) can be linked to international outsourcing. After all, this very outsourcing is why advanced producer services are needed to produce these capabilities so that multinationals' headquarters can manage their globally-dispersed production process. This is also why these services cluster in global cities. The activities of the accountants, consultants, lawyers, financial specialists, and the like who are involved with this production can consequently be linked to international outsourcing. Given that this only concerns an element of the employment in producer services in a global city, the impact of international outsourcing on the economic base of cities in the advanced economies in general is minimal.

As argued and demonstrated, nationally or regionally oriented cities can also have a very substantial part of their employment in the producer services. These services are, however, by definition not involved in producing the capability for the headquarters of multinationals to manage their globally-dispersed production process. Consider, for instance, Utrecht, whose economic base when it comes to employment in manufacturing and advanced producer services closely resembles that of the global city of Amsterdam (compare Figure 2.2), but instead functions as 'the centre of *nationally oriented* producer services' (Ministry of Economic Affairs, 2004; italics added). This is completely in accordance with Sassen's claim that the clustering of advanced producer services 'exists in cities that function as regional nodes – that is, at smaller geographical scales and lower levels of complexity than global cities' (Sassen, 2006a: 193; cf. Friedmann, 1995: 22, Sassen, 2000: 139, 2006c: x, 2012: 323). However, in such 'regional nodes', there is no clear link with international outsourcing. This is already explicitly referred to in this quote, which mentions the smaller geographical scales on which the driving processes occur. In practice, this means that national or regional, instead of global, forces may also drive the clustering of advanced producer services in the bulk of cities in the advanced economies. Indeed, this is why they are labelled as regional nodes in the first place.

Yet, in the global city debate, the clustering of advanced producer services in all cities in the advanced economies is still considered to be a consequence of international outsourcing. A recent study in this debate speaks volumes on this matter. Zhong, Clark, and Sassen aimed to assess 'globalization impacts on changes in income inequality' (2007: 385) by rigorously testing the polarization thesis by comparing more than 250 cities in the United States. In their study, the 'share of earnings by producer services' was considered to be, and was used as, a 'globalization variable' (Zhong et al., 2007: 387). The argument for doing this is, unsurprisingly given that Sassen is one of the authors, in accordance with the global city theoretical framework: 'producer services like finance, accounting, internet consulting, and law firms are critical to support other global businesses' (2007: 387). In short, producer services facilitate the management of the new international division of labour brought about by international outsourcing. Yet, although this might be true for some of the producer services in global cities like New York, the bulk of the 250 cities in Zhong et al.'s study will, at most, function as regional nodes. Consequently, the link with international outsourcing simply does not exist for the producer services located there. Modelling producer services as a globalization variable therefore seems to be way off course, and will consequently greatly overestimate the impact of economic globalization on urban labour markets.

2.5 Conclusions

In the global city debate, it is often assumed that the economic base of cities in the advanced economies becomes similar to that of global cities. This produces the standard research practice of interpreting the impact of economic globalization on labour markets in cities in general on the basis of the theoretical notions of the global city theoretical framework. However, the assumption that all cities will become similar to global cities could be in doubt, as the global city theoretical framework asserts two other scenarios concerning the growth of advanced producer services. This is why this chapter addressed the research question: *Does the economic base of cities in general increasingly resemble the economic base of global cities?*

This chapter demonstrates that this question needs to be answered in the negative. This is because the economic base of many Dutch cities did not increasingly resemble that of the global city of Amsterdam between 1995 and 2008, by and large because Dutch cities diverged when it came to the employment shares in the advanced producer services. Indeed, they did so in accordance with Sassen's arguments on this factor. She argued that the clustering of advanced producer services in the most service-oriented cities, most notably global cities and regional nodes, feeds on the deindustrialization of former industrial strongholds. The fact that the employment share in manufacturing declined in all Dutch cities, while in the most service-oriented cities the employment share in the advanced producer services grew much faster than in the most industrial places, also points in that direction. Moreover, the findings suggest that in addition to this scenario of predatory growth, one of double predatory growth is occurring as well, i.e. the growth of advanced producer services in global cities like Amsterdam at the cost of that growth in other service-oriented economies. All of the above indicates that the economic base of many Dutch cities therefore decreasingly, instead of increasingly, resembled that of the global city of Amsterdam in the assessed time period.

This is contrary to what is often assumed in the global city debate, and is in contrast to Mollenkopf's recent claim that 'the economic functions that are concentrated in global cities – that some scholars think distinguish them from other, lesser cities – are growing relatively faster outside the big central cities and in metropolitan areas lower down the national and international hierarchy' (Mollenkopf, 2009: 273). In reality, at least in the Netherlands, the opposite is the case: the clustering in the advanced producer services was strongest in the most service-oriented cities, especially in the global city of Amsterdam. That Mollenkopf cautions against using the global city theoretical rationale for cities lower down the urban hierarchy in a section entitled 'some terms do not travel well' (2009: 272-4) is right on the money. Certainly, on the basis of my findings, such caution does indeed seem to be justified. However, given Mollenkopf's convergence claim, the opposite line of reasoning, i.e. that 'some terms do travel well', would have been more appropriate.

The findings in this chapter reveal that the economic base of all cities in the advanced economies does not necessarily become similar to that of global cities in the current phase of economic globalization. Certainly, this did not happen in the Netherlands where, between 1995 and 2008, many cities became less similar to the global city of Amsterdam. Furthermore, Kasarda and Friedrichs came to similar conclusions in the 1980s with respect to cities in the United States and West Germany, respectively (1985, 1986). All of this suggests that predatory growth is occurring in the advanced economies in general. Accordingly, contrary to what is often claimed, global cities do not display the future guise of cities lower down the urban hierarchy (e.g. Burgers, 1996; Mollenkopf, 2009; Mollenkopf

& Castells, 1992; Vaattovaara & Kortteinen, 2003). In the idiom used by Dangschat (1994), some cities 'win' while others 'lose' in the transition to a post-industrial economy, with the former being cities that were already service-oriented in the 1970s, while the latter are, most notably, former industrial strongholds. Applying the global city theoretical framework as a universal prism of interpretation for detecting the impact of globalization on cities in general is therefore highly problematic, particularly if another invalid assumption in the global city debate that was addressed in this chapter is taken into account.

According to the global city theoretical framework, international outsourcing induces the deindustrialization and clustering of advanced producer services in cities in the advanced economies. As the bulk of research findings on these matters point in another direction, the second research question addressed in this chapter was: *Does international outsourcing drive deindustrialization and the clustering of advanced producer services in cities?* Although this clustering in global cities is partly driven by international outsourcing, in so far as it concerns the advanced producer services that produce 'the capabilities for servicing, managing, and financing the global operations of firms and markets' (Sassen, 2001: 359; cf. Sassen, 1991, 2006a, 2006d, 2012), the link between clustering and international outsourcing seems to be missing in cities that function as regional nodes. Instead, the clustering of advanced producer services in these nodes is driven by national or regional processes. For the Dutch case, this means that only part of the employment growth in the advanced producer services in the global city of Amsterdam is indeed driven by international outsourcing. Just as claimed in the global city theoretical framework, those advanced producer services produce the inputs that the headquarters of multinationals located in this global city need to coordinate their globally-dispersed production processes. They can thus be linked to economic globalization. Yet, other service-oriented Dutch cities like Utrecht primarily function as national or regional nodes, and the link between the clustering of advanced producer services and global economic restructuring in the form of international outsourcing in those cities thus seems to be absent. This suggests that several studies on the global city debate have so far overestimated the impact of economic globalization on urban labour demand, as they mapped this effect by assessing the consequences of the clustering of advanced producer services. Certainly, many of these studies assessed this impact on cities that function as global cities (see Table A1 in Appendix A). Yet, others included former industrial strongholds and/or cities that are more likely to function as regional nodes.

That said, it needs to be emphasized that I do not disqualify large-scale comparisons like those made by Zhong, Clark, and Sassen (2007), where the bulk of cities are by definition former industrial strongholds and regional nodes. On the contrary, I applaud such a systematic approach for rigorously testing the polarization thesis, as 'comparing many locations has the advantages of (1) offering greater variations on key hypothesized variables and (2) controlling impacts of other variables that may generate spurious results in a few cases' (Zhong, Clark & Sassen, 2007: 386). Consequently, such comparative frameworks are a valuable contribution to the global city debate, in which the bulk of research concerns case studies of one or two cities that lack such rigor. Yet, the very irony is that by using such a framework the findings are falsely attributed to international outsourcing, and the new international division of labour that stems from it, *if the share of employment in the advanced producer services is used as a globalization indicator.* This does not mean that such a research framework should be abandoned altogether, as this would mean throwing the baby out with the bathwater. Indeed, rigorous testing of the polarization (and professionalization) thesis needs such a comparative framework, as claimed by Zhong, Clark, and Sassen (2007). Accordingly, using this type of framework is a great step forward in the global city debate. However, if such a framework is combined with the operationalization of economic globalization and/or international outsourcing by means of the share of employment in the advanced producer services, it will greatly overestimate the impact of this globalization and/or outsourcing. This is because the bulk of the employment in those services in former industrial strongholds and regional nodes has no relation to international outsourcing whatsoever.

3 Advanced producer services and labour demand

The structure of economic activity has brought about changes in the organization of work that are reflected in a pronounced shift in the job-supply, with strong polarization occurring in the (…) occupational distribution of workers (Sassen, 2006a: 197).

Sassen's thesis of growing social polarisation in global cities is flawed [because] it fails to engage adequately with existing work on social change, and the evidence of large-scale professionalisation in the occupational structure of Western societies and many global cities (Hamnett, 1994a: 422).

Studies of the city traditionally posit a division between a city's economy and its culture, with culture subordinate in explanatory power to 'work' (Clark et al., 2003: 291).

3.1 Introduction

This chapter aims to assess the empirical validity of two competing theories in the global city debate on urban labour demand: the polarization and professionalization theses. The former essentially argues that the clustering of advanced producer services leads to an hourglass-shaped urban occupational hierarchy, with a high demand for labour for both the highest and lowest occupational strata. Consequently, this thesis predicts that in cities with the highest employment shares in the advanced producer services, the occupational hierarchy will be the most strongly polarized; and these cities will thus have the smallest mismatch between labour demand and supply at the bottom of the labour market.

The professionalization thesis, on the other hand, argues that the clustering of advanced producer services leads to *high* labour demand for the highest occupational stratum and *low* labour demand for the lowest. In terms of the former outcome, the polarization and professionalization theses do not, therefore, differ. However, the crucial difference between them is that professionalization theory predicts that cities with the greatest share of employment in the advanced producer services have to cope with the largest, instead of the smallest, mismatch between labour demand and supply at the bottom of the labour market.

Section 3.2 will elaborate on the theoretical arguments of the polarization and professionalization theses, while Section 3.3 will assess their empirical validity when it comes to explaining the labour demand for less-educated urbanites. Thereafter, the findings will be interpreted in Section 3.4 in light of the theorizing on the role of the consumption base of cities initiated by Richard Florida (2002, 2003, 2004, 2005). This theorizing turns the productivist logic of theorizing in the global city debate on its head by claiming that the settlement of advanced producer services is determined by the lifestyle-driven residential preferences of the professionals they employ. In short: 'capital follows labour' instead of the other way round. If this is correct, the production base of cities is derived from their consumption base (shorthand: consumerist perspective), instead of the other way round, as Sassen and Hamnett claim (shorthand: productivist perspective). Section 3.5, meanwhile, empirically disentangles these two perspectives in an attempt to discover whether the impact of the advanced producer services on the employment of less-educated urbanites needs to be interpreted according to the former or latter viewpoint. Finally, the concluding Section, 3.6, discusses the findings of this chapter and answers the following research question: *What is the impact of the clustering of advanced producer services on the unemployment rate of less-educated urbanites?*

3.2 Polarization, professionalization and mismatch

3.2.1 The polarization thesis

The polarization thesis in urban studies is clearly influenced by Braverman, who argued that the rise of the service economy leads to proletarianization due to automation and de-skilling (1974). Consequently, in the transition to a post-industrial economy, the intermediate occupational categories that are characteristic of the industrial era wither away, leading to an hourglass-shaped occupational hierarchy of highly-educated professionals at the top and a less-educated service proletariat at the bottom.

Braverman's thesis was formulated for the transition to a service economy at the country level, but Friedmann and Wolff (1982), Noyelle (1983), Sassen (Sassen-Koob, 1984a, 1984b, 1986), and Trachte and Ross (1985) were the first to apply it to occupational change in urban economies. It is, however, in particular the work of Sassen (1991, 2001) on global cities that stirred discussions on the alleged polarization of urban labour markets in the global city debate. Predominantly, the chapters *Employment and Earnings* and *Class and Spatial Polarization* in the first (1991) and second (2001) editions of *The Global City* have become the main point of reference in this debate. Furthermore, the central arguments in these chapters have remained unchanged (Sassen, 2006a, 2007, 2012).

Sassen asserts that the combination of deindustrialization and the clustering of advanced producer services leads to the polarization of the occupational hierarchy (Sassen-Koob, 1984a, 1984b, 1985, 1986; Sassen, 1991, 2000, 2001, 2006a, 2007, 2012). The theoretical rationale behind this polarization is that 'different types of economic growth promote different types of social forms. In the post-World War II era, growth was characterized by the vast expansion of a middle class (...) The historical forms assumed by this expansion, notably capital intensity, standardization, and suburbanization (...) acted against the casualization of work' (2001: 255). In the current global age, this process is more or less inverted: '[T]he group of service industries that were one of the driving economic forces beginning in the 1980s [the advanced producer services, JvdW], and continue as such today, is characterized by greater (...) *occupational dispersion*, weak unions, and a *growing share of casualized low-wage jobs*' (Sassen, 2006a: 173, italics added; cf. 2012: 243). According to the polarization thesis, there are two mechanisms by which the occupational hierarchy in global cities will become dispersed, i.e. polarized, due to the clustering of advanced producer services.

The first of these is often referred to as a 'direct effect', because it concerns employment in the firms that produce services: 'Almost half the jobs in the producer services are lower-income jobs, and the other half are in the two highest earning classes' (Sassen, 2006a: 197; cf. 2000: 142, 2012: Chapter 6). The former are the less-educated facilitators such as cleaners, clerks, and security, while the latter are well-educated professionals like financial specialists, accountants, and consultants, who perform complex operations (Sassen, 2000: 142, 2006a: 197, 2012: Chapter 6). A growing share of advanced producer services in cities therefore increases labour demand at both the top and bottom of the occupational hierarchy.

The second mechanism is often referred to as an 'indirect' or 'multiplier effect' (cf. Burgers & Musterd, 2002: 409). It is driven by the consumption pattern that the well-educated professionals employed in the advanced producer services need to maintain to enable their 24/7 working lives. This pattern is supposed to yield demand for 'an army of low-wage workers (...) including residential building attendants, dog-walkers, housekeepers for the two-career family, workers in the gourmet restaurants and food shops, French hand laundries, and so on' (Sassen-Koob, 1985: 262; cf. Sassen-Koob, 1984a, 1984b, 1986; Sassen, 1988, 2001, 2006a, 2012). However, it also refers to both workers in a downgraded manufacturing sector that is directed at limited runs of customized production, and employees in small specialist retail outlets offering limited edition consumer goods (Sassen-Koob, 1984b, 1986; Sassen, 1993).

According to the polarization thesis, then, the occupational hierarchy that characterized an urban economy in the industrial regime, also referred to as the Fordist era, was onion-shaped: large in the middle and small at the top and bottom. In the current post-industrial/post-Fordist era, however, in which the clustering of advanced producer services is considered to be the driving force of employment growth, this onion-shaped industrial occupational hierarchy gives way to a post-industrial version that is hourglass-shaped, i.e. small in the middle and large at the top and bottom. The polarization thesis has thus been conceived of as 'the theory of the declining middle' (Fainstein, 2002). If this is correct, the smallest mismatch between labour demand and supply at the bottom of Dutch urban labour markets exists in cities with the highest share of advanced producer services, due to the aforementioned direct and indirect labour demand for low-skilled service workers that is the result of the clustering of advanced producer services.

The first of the two crucial hypotheses that can be derived from the polarization thesis, and which will be tested in this chapter, states that *the unemployment rate of less-educated urbanites is lowest in cities with the highest employment shares in the advanced producer services* (Hypothesis 1 – the direct effect). According to polarization theory, part of the impact of the advanced producer services on the unemployment rates of less-educated urbanites is the result of the previously mentioned indirect labour demand in the consumer services that cater to the professionals employed in the advanced producer services. The second hypothesis therefore maintains that *the negative impact of employment in the advanced producer services on the unemployment rate of less-educated urbanites can partly be attributed to the employment share in the hotel and catering industry* (Hypothesis 2 – the indirect effect).[3]

3 In line with Sassen's polarization thesis, it would be optimal if the impact of the share of employment in private households could also be modelled. Unfortunately, data on that share are unavailable at the metropolitan level in the Netherlands. Furthermore, the metropolitan-level data do not enable employment to be modelled in: 1) a downgraded manufacturing sector directed at limited runs of customized production, and 2) small specialist retail outlets offering limited editions of 'hipster' consumer goods. This is because these kinds of employment cannot be empirically disentangled in the data available at the metropolitan level from: a) large-scale mass production, and b) large-scale wholesale and retail trade.

3.2.2 The professionalization thesis

Chris Hamnett has formulated the most prominent critique of the polarization thesis in the global city debate. Hamnett's claim is that the occupational hierarchy of global cities will become professionalized instead of polarized. More specifically, he suggests that the transition to a post-industrial urban economy leads to professionalization, because the post-industrial occupational hierarchy is more professionalized than the industrial version. The crucial difference with polarization theory is that, according to the professionalization thesis, the clustering of advanced producer services leads to high labour demand for the highest occupational stratum, but *low* labour demand for the lowest occupational level.

Hamnett's seminal work, which sparked the 'polarization versus professionalization dispute', contains two arguments, which he has repeated ever since, as to why he expects professionalization instead of polarization in global cities (1996a, 1996b, 1998, 2004). Hamnett's first reason for doubting the polarization thesis is because it has already been challenged at the national level. In particular, in 1997, Wright and Martin found that the transition to a post-industrial economy led to professionalization instead of proletarianization in the United States in the 1970s (for Europe, see: Esping-Andersen, 1993). Accordingly, using the terminology of the issue at hand, the transition to a post-industrial economy leads to low, not high, labour demand for the less educated in the United States. This finding does, however, stem from a country-level study, and is therefore not necessarily incompatible with Sassen's polarization thesis on cities.

Hamnett's second argument as to why Sassen's polarization theory is erroneous is more relevant to this study; he considers it to be 'American-centric', as Sassen bases her claims on the occupational hierarchy of New York and other major cities in the United States, such as Los Angeles. Hamnett, however, does not believe that these cities are representative of global cities in general, as they combine a high influx of immigrants with a deregulated labour market. As a result, a high labour demand for low-skilled service workers can be met by a large supply of cheap, low-skilled labour. This combination does not exist in most advanced economies, because they are more regulated and/or attract fewer low-skilled immigrants than New York and Los Angeles do. As a consequence, a growing low-wage service sector might not be a 'universal' feature of global cities, but an exceptionality of global cities in the United States.

In short, according to Hamnett, global cities in more regulated economies, such as on the European mainland, are more prone to professionalize than polarize, due to the clustering of advanced producer services, especially when the share of immigrants in the population is not as high as in New York or Los Angeles. According to this reasoning, then, the clustering of advanced producer services leads to high labour demand for the better educated, but low demand for their less well educated counterparts. If this is correct, the greatest mismatch between labour demand and supply at the bottom of the Dutch urban labour market exists in cities with the highest share of advanced producer services. The crucial hypothesis that can be derived from the professionalization thesis therefore is *the unemployment rate of less-educated urbanites is highest in cities with the highest employment shares in the advanced producer services* (Hypothesis 3).

3.2.3 Polarization and professionalization in Dutch cities

Burgers and Musterd (2002) have previously applied the polarization and professionalization theses to the two biggest cities in the Netherlands, Amsterdam and Rotterdam (2002). To do this, they divided total urban employment into a Fordist and post-Fordist occupational hierarchy according to the classification scheme of Esping-Andersen (1993). This is particularly appropriate for the question at hand, 'because it relates inequality directly to economic restructuring. Thus, it can be easily related to the theoretical notions of Sassen (...). As a case in point, Sassen's claim of social polarization resulting from the growing service character of urban economies should be especially visible in the "post-Fordist" job hierarchy' (Burgers & Musterd, 2002: 408). In assessments of the empirical validity of the polarization and professionalization theses in the global city debate, it has consequently become standard research practice to use this classification scheme (e.g. Buck, 1997; Hamnett, 1994a, 1994b, 1996a, 2004; Rhein, 1996; Steijn, Snel & Van der Laan, 2000).

Burgers and Musterd found that 'both cities show a continuing deindustrialization of their local economy during the first half of the 1990s. But because this occurred at a much slower pace in Rotterdam than in Amsterdam, the relative difference between the two cities has increased in this respect. [Consequently,] the difference between Amsterdam and Rotterdam as to the share of Fordist (and thus of post-Fordist) jobs has almost doubled (...) between 1992 and 1996' (2002: 408). This is not particularly surprising given the finding in the previous chapter that Amsterdam is the most post-industrial (in Burgers and Musterd's terminology, post-Fordist) Dutch city, where the share of employment in the advanced producer services has increased more strongly than in any other city (see Figures 2.2 and 2.4).

Burgers and Musterd's (2002) comparison of the post-Fordist occupational hierarchy in Amsterdam with that in Rotterdam demonstrated that the former fits the polarization model, and the latter the professionalization model. In Amsterdam, the transition to a post-industrial economy led to a high demand for labour for both the highly and the less educated. In Rotterdam, on the other hand, it only led to a high labour demand for the former group. According to Burgers and Musterd (2002), this finding is responsible for the fact that the unemployment rate of less-educated urbanites in Rotterdam is substantially higher than that in Amsterdam. That 'Sassen's polarization model seems to be more powerful in explaining inequality in Amsterdam while the mismatch scheme (...) seems more adequate for Rotterdam' (409) is subsequently interpreted according to the theoretical reasoning of the polarization thesis. It is suggested that the greater share of professionals in the advanced producer services in Amsterdam compared to Rotterdam is what drives the higher labour demand for low-skilled service workers in the former than in the latter: 'As Sassen has suggested, the presence of the new middle class – itself largely the result of an expanding service sector – in turn creates additional employment in the service sector, mainly in those parts which cater for the lifestyles of these urban professionals: restaurants, specialty shops, cultural industries and so forth' (ibid.).

However, the question of whether employment in the advanced producer services really is responsible for the high labour demand for low-skilled workers, as claimed in the polarization thesis, is as yet unanswered. The same also applies to the issue of whether this occurs through the direct and indirect effects that this thesis entails. Indeed, a simple comparison of Amsterdam with Rotterdam cannot alone determine the validity of this suggested cause.

3.3 Assessing the impact of advanced producer services on labour demand

The claim of several scholars in the global city debate that a global city like Amsterdam wears the future guise of cities lower down the urban hierarchy did not stand the test set out in the previous chapter. Although all 22 Dutch metropolitan areas did become less industrial, their economic base did not become like that of the global city of Amsterdam. On the contrary, in the most service-oriented cities, the employment share in the advanced producer services saw a greater increase than in former industrial strongholds. In combination with the findings of Burgers and Musterd that the occupational hierarchy of Amsterdam is polarized, while it is professionalized in Rotterdam (2002), this suggests that in cities with the highest employment share in the advanced producer services, the occupational hierarchy will be polarized. In contrast, it will be professionalized in cities with a low employment share in these services, and these cities will thus have to deal with a mismatch between labour demand and supply at the bottom of the labour market.

This all seems to be in accordance with a crucial hypothesis that can be deduced from the polarization thesis in the global city theoretical framework: in cities with the highest share of advanced producer services the mismatch between labour demand and supply at the bottom of the labour market is the lowest (Hypothesis 1 – direct effect), and this can partly be explained by the employment share in the hotel and catering industry (Hypothesis 2 – indirect effect). Table 3.1 assesses whether these claims are correct by modelling the impact of the employment shares in the advanced producer services and hotel and catering industry on the unemployment rate of less-educated urbanites in the 22 Dutch metropolitan areas (see Appendix B for a detailed description of the datasets used in this study and the operationalization of the variables).[4] As the data used have a multilevel structure, twelve years within 22 cities, multilevel modelling is required (Hox, 1995). Consequently, Table 3.1 starts with a null model, which shows how much variation there is in *unemployment rate less educated* at the level of metropolitan areas, and how much of this variation exists at the level of years. The null model indicates that 35.9% (0.90 / (0.90 + 1.61) of the variation in the unemployment rate of the less educated occurs because urban economies differ, while 64.1% (1.61 / (0.90 + 1.61)) of this variation results from fluctuations in time, probably as a result of the economic boom in the second half of the 1990s and the economic bust after 2001.

In addition to the variable *age 15-24*, which is used to control for the demographic make-up of cities, I entered the variable *producer services* in Model 1 in an attempt to discover whether cities with the highest share of producer services have the lowest (polarization thesis / Hypothesis 1) or highest (professionalization thesis / Hypothesis 3) share of unemployment

4 As the calculation of the variable *unemployment rate less educated* gave reason to suspect that it underestimates what it aims to measure, all the analyses with that variable have been replicated with a variable that measures the general unemployment rate. These replications or 'robustness checks' are reported in Appendix D.

among their less-educated citizens.[5] The negative and significant coefficient of *producer services* confirms the former hypothesis, which is deduced from the polarization thesis, and rejects the latter, which is surmised from the professionalization thesis.[6] This suggests that there is both polarization and professionalization in Dutch cities, just as Burgers and Musterd demonstrated for Amsterdam and Rotterdam (2002), albeit under different conditions. The former applies to the most service-oriented cities in the Netherlands, while the latter applies to the most industrial cities, which consequently have to deal with a mismatch between labour demand and supply at the bottom of the urban labour market. This can be interpreted according to the argument of polarization theory, as the clustering of advanced producer services proved to be crucial for explaining the extent to which such a mismatch occurs in cities. In cities with the highest share of advanced producer services, the unemployment rate for less-educated urbanites is at its lowest, and not at its highest, as claimed by the professionalization thesis.

5 To help with the readability of this study, all regression analyses will be presented as elegantly as possible. This means that they will be as concise as possible, which is achieved by only including the essential variables. Please note, however, that previous studies over a somewhat shorter period (1998-2007 instead of 1996-2007) on the impact of the employment share in the advanced producer services on the unemployment rates of less-educated urbanites in Dutch cities, which included more control variables, did yield similar results (Van der Waal & Burgers, 2011; Van der Waal, 2012, 2013b). These studies included control variables such as the share of less-educated urbanites and the size of the working population, and these did not produce different findings than the ones reported in this study when it comes to the corroboration or refutation of hypotheses. In addition, the analyses reported in this research have also been performed with those additional control variables (not reported), but this did not alter the central findings. This means that the same hypotheses were corroborated or refuted. This all suggests that the findings reported in this study on the basis of concise models are robust.

6 The variance of *unemployment rate less educated* at the year level declines, as might be expected, but the variance at the metropolitan level increases after entering *producer services* and the control variable. This seems to be rather odd, as entering variables normally leads to a fall in the variance of the dependent variable. However, in multilevel modelling, the opposite sometimes happens, which indicates the omission of important explanatory variables in the model (Kreft & De Leeuw, 1998). It thus simply means that as well as the clustering of advanced producer services, there are other important factors that also determine the unemployment rate of the less educated in Dutch cities. In the chapters to come, we will see whether these important factors include the ones hypothesized by the theoretical notions under scrutiny in this study.

Table 3.1 Unemployment rate of the less educated in the 22 Dutch metropolitan areas (1996-2007), explained by the employment shares in the advanced producer services, and the hotel and catering industry (multilevel regression analysis; entries are regression coefficients; estimation: maximum likelihood)

	Null model	Model 1	Model 2
Independents	*B*	*B*	*B*
Constant	4.62***	11.41***	11.50***
Advanced producer services		-0.22***	-0.22***
Hotel and catering industry			-0.04
Controls			
Age 15-24		-0.17**	-0.17**
Variance metropolitan level ($N = 22$)	0.90	1.46	1.45
Variance year level ($N = 12$)	1.61	1.49	1.49
Log likelihood	-518.09	-507.97	-507.96

Source: StatLine CBS (own calculations)
*$p < 0.05$; **$p < 0.01$; ***$p < 0.001$

Figure 3.1 depicts this finding. Its horizontal axis indicates the employment share in the advanced producer services, while the vertical axis sets out the unemployment rate of less-educated urbanites. The line represents that rate, as predicted on the basis of Model 2 in Table 3.1, while the grey area indicates the confidence intervals. Clearly, the predicted unemployment rate is lowest (highest) in cities with the highest (lowest) employment share in the advanced producer services. In the case of an urban economy with an employment share in the advanced producer services of 13% (the lowest score in the dataset used), an unemployment rate of 6.54% is predicted among less-educated urbanites. Meanwhile, in a city with 33% of its total employment in those services (the highest score in the dataset used), an unemployment rate of 2.08% is predicted for these urbanites. The latter unemployment rate is three times lower than the former. It should be noted however – as elaborated on in Note 2 and Appendix D – that these unemployment scores are probably underestimations. The robustness check in Appendix D yields more likely estimates of unemployment rates. This indicates that in the city with the lowest employment share in the advanced producer services, the predicted unemployment rate is 9.5%, while it is predicted to be 1.9% in the city with the highest share of that type of employment. It can thus be concluded that the former unemployment rate is almost five times higher than the latter (see Figure D1 in Appendix D).

Figure 3.1 Unemployment rate of less-educated urbanites as predicted by the employment shares in the advanced producer services in the 22 Dutch metropolitan areas

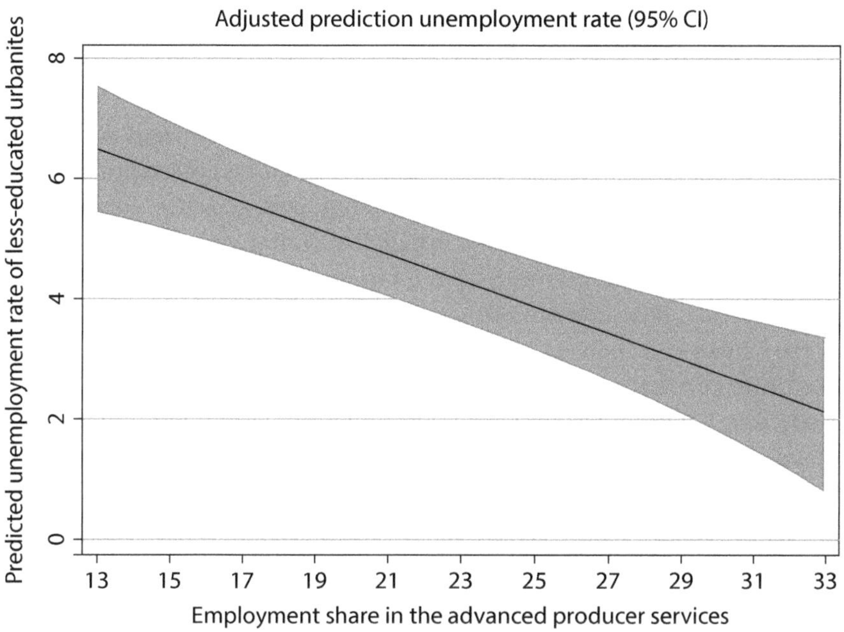

Although the impact of the advanced producer services on the unemployment rate of less-educated urbanites is clearly in line with Sassen's polarization thesis, Model 2 of Table 3.1 indicates that Dutch urban labour markets do not totally function according to that theory. Indeed, Model 2 demonstrates that the employment share in the hotel and catering industry does not negatively affect those unemployment rates, unlike what would be expected on the basis of the polarization thesis. This employment share can thus not even be partly responsible for the negative impact of the advanced producer services on the unemployment of less-educated urbanites. This suggests that polarization theory's prediction that the indirect labour demand in the consumer services due to the consumption pattern of the professionals employed in the advanced producer services does not occur, or cannot account for city-level differences in unemployment, in the Netherlands. This means that Hypothesis 2 must be rejected. The concluding section of this chapter will elaborate further on this finding. However, there first needs to be scrutiny of whether Sassen's productivist interpretation of the impact of the advanced producer services on unemployment, which has been corroborated in this section, holds true when confronted with a consumerist alternative.

3.4 A consumerist alternative: cultural amenities and the demand for low-skilled labour

Although the theoretical logic of the polarization and professionalization theses outlined and scrutinized in the previous sections gained prominence from the early 1990s onwards, when it comes to understanding labour market opportunities for less-educated urbanites, an alternative can be deduced from the more recent literature that focuses on the consumption, instead of production, base of post-industrial cities. The scholarly attention paid to the causes and consequences of the local production and consumption of culture and the arts has increased considerably in recent years (cf. Aoyama, 2009; Clark, 2003a; Currid, 2010; Glaeser, 2011; Musterd & Murie, 2010; Musterd & Kovacs, 2013). Notwithstanding the broad range of topics covered by those studies, their common denominator is the assumption that the growing salience of cultural amenities in many cities underlies economic development. That denominator challenges production-based notions of urban economic development, which focus on the production of goods and services for non-local markets. As Aoyama puts it: '[G]eographic variations across cities have long been explained through processes of production, and seldom through processes of consumption', while 'consumption has become the most prominent feature of postindustrial urban space' (2009: 341; cf. Markusen & Schrock, 2009: 344).

Whether consumption is indeed the most prominent feature of post-industrial cities today remains an empirical question, but the notion that it plays a vital role in urban development has an increasing number of proponents. About ten years ago, Clark also prompted other scholars in the field of urban studies to take consumption and entertainment seriously, as 'old paradigms – such as "land, labor, capital, and management generate economic development" – are too simple' (2003a: 1). Furthermore, after critically scrutinizing studies that focus on production-base explanations, Markusen and Schrock recently emphasized 'that the consumption base of urban regions, i.e. goods and services that are locally produced and locally consumed, can also be a source of regional job growth and stability' (2009: 344). These ideas and findings provide a stepping stone for developing a consumption-based alternative to the production-based explanation provided by Sassen's polarization thesis for the varying unemployment rates across post-industrial cities.

These ideas do this because the cultural industries, just like the advanced producer services, might also yield a high demand for less-educated labour by way of two mechanisms. The first of these is that those industries are likely to employ a substantial number of low-skilled workers to facilitate their main processes. Just like office buildings, many cultural activities require cleaning and security, while, of course, the visitors those activities attract also need to be catered for (thus: the direct effect in the consumerist perspective; cf. Clark, 2003b; Florida, 2004).

The second mechanism that relates cultural amenities to demand for a less-educated labour-force is the consumption pattern of the professionals employed in the cultural industries. This is because it is suggested that their 'propensity to spend locally is high, because of the structure of their preferences' (Markusen & Schrock, 2009: 345). More specifically, it is assumed that the consumption pattern of the professionals employed in the cultural industries roughly mirrors that of their counterparts in the advanced producer services, yielding a high demand for personal services and the hotel and catering industry (i.e. the indirect effect in the consumerist perspective). However, this interpretation is radically different, as that consumption pattern is not considered to be a necessary condition for maintaining a 24/7 working life, which is the argument in the polarization thesis, but a lifestyle-driven phenomenon and identity marker. Nevertheless, although both mechanisms in the consumerist perspective provide an additional, alternative explanation to the two mechanisms provided by polarization theory for the varying unemployment rates of the lower-educated across cities, all four can coexist. It could, however, also very well be that the former two mechanisms might (partly) account for the variation in those unemployment rates that has been attributed in the previous section to the latter two mechanisms.

Firstly, this is because cities that are renowned for what they have to offer in terms of culture and the arts, almost without exception, also stand out as hubs for advanced producer services; take, for instance, New York, London, Paris, and Amsterdam. Furthermore, studies on the United States have demonstrated that these anecdotal empirical observations are indicative of a more general pattern: cities with high employment shares in the advanced producer services are also the ones that are rich in cultural amenities, and this does not just apply to the usual suspects at the top of the urban hierarchy mentioned above (Currid & Connolly, 2008; Florida, 2003, 2005). This suggests that the employment effects of the clustering of advanced producer services at the bottom of urban labour markets, as theorized in the polarization thesis, may be overstated: the demand for low-skilled workers might (partly) stem from the local cultural consumption base, as implied by the theory on cultural amenities developed in this section. This would mean that the negative impact of the employment share in the advanced producer services on the unemployment rate of less-educated urbanites, which was identified in the previous section, might (partly) be the result of the impact on that unemployment of the employment share in the cultural industries. As a consequence, to produce a good estimation of the former impact, it needs to be modelled simultaneously with the latter impact.

Secondly, Richard Florida goes one step further than just emphasizing that cultural consumption can, in itself, be important for urban economic development by claiming that the causal direction between labour and capital flows has been radically reversed in the post-industrial era (2002, 2003, 2004, 2005). Whereas the productivist claim is that people settle in places with ample job opportunities, Florida states that many service-production firms locate where young knowledge workers prefer to live. This idea amounts to the consumerist explanation for the varying unemployment rates across cities, as Florida also argues that these workers prefer to live in cities that are rich in cultural amenities (cf. Glaeser et al., 2001; Glaeser et al., 2003; Currid, 2010). This is not just a theoretical expectation; the share of college graduates in the population is high in cities with an abundance of 'constructed amenities, like the numbers of opera, research libraries, used and rare books stores, juice bars, Starbucks, and bicycle events' (Clark, 2003b: 132).

The previously demonstrated substantial, positive relationship between the advanced producer services and cultural amenities, and Florida's claim that these services settle in places that are rich in such amenities, both indicate that the polarization thesis's previous interpretations of the varying demand for less-educated labour across cities in the advanced economies might be overstated (see, in addition to the previous section: Elliott, 1999a, 2004; Kasarda, 1985; Kasarda & Friedrichs, 1985; Van der Waal, 2010, 2012, 2013b; Van der Waal & Burgers, 2009, 2011). More specifically, for two reasons, the low unemployment rate among less-educated urbanites in cities with a high share of advanced producer services might (partly) be the result of the consumption base of those cities, i.e. the cultural industries, instead of, as previously assumed, their production base.

The first reason relates to the fact that previous interpretations by those relying on the polarization thesis (partly) rest on a spurious relationship, due to the very positive relationship between cultural amenities and advanced producer services. (Part of) the relationship between unemployment rates and employment levels in the advanced producer services might thus be the result of the presence of cultural amenities, as theorized in this section. Secondly, (part) of the effect of the advanced producer services is ultimately driven by the presence of cultural amenities, as it is these amenities that underlie the settlement of these services, as first argued by Florida. Accordingly, to assess the empirical validity of both the productivist polarization theory for explaining varying unemployment rates across cities and the consumerist alternative developed in this section, the two explanations need to be modelled simultaneously, which will be described below. Such an assessment does, however, call for the modelling of a third explanation for the strong relation between the presence of advanced producer services and cultural amenities might be the result of agglomeration economies.

Contrary to what was expected on the basis of both the classic labour-follows-capital explanation and Florida's capital-follows-labour version, advanced producer services and cultural amenities might also be related because both of them, for various and different reasons, can reap the economic benefits of the mere size of a city, such as knowledge spillovers, a large supply of consumers, a good infrastructure (Fujita & Thisse, 2002), and information and communication loops (Storper & Venables, 2004). Although the precise mechanisms by which advanced producer services and cultural industries will benefit from settlement within the largest cities are not the focus of this study, disentangling the causal relationship between the presence of those services and industries mentioned above at least calls for controlling for agglomeration economies. It may be that the previously demonstrated relationship between the two is not because one results from the other, but because both are the result of agglomeration economies and can, therefore, particularly be found in the largest cities. Even if they are not causally related, this would explain a strong relationship between advanced producer services and cultural amenities.

Figure 3.2 illustrates the conceptual model that integrates the theoretical arguments outlined above. The left-hand side depicts the expectations on the basis of agglomeration effects. The vertical vector on this side indicates the expectation deduced from Florida's consumerist notion that the growth of the advanced producer services is caused by the presence of cultural industries (Hypothesis 4). The vertical vector on the right-hand side represents the expectation surmised from the classic labour-follows-capital or productivist notion that cultural industries thrive in places with high employment shares in the advanced producer services (Hypothesis 5).

The upper right-hand side of Figure 1 represents the polarization thesis as it was tested in the previous section. This predicts that the advanced producer services have a direct negative effect on the unemployment rate

Figure 3.2 The expected impact of 1) the working population on the advanced producer services, cultural industries, and hotel and catering industry (agglomeration effect), 2) the advanced producer services on the cultural industries and/or vice versa (production-driven and/or consumption-driven settlement), and 3) the advanced producer services (polarization thesis, or production-based explanation) and cultural industries (thesis on cultural amenities, or consumption-based explanation) on the unemployment rate of less-educated urbanites

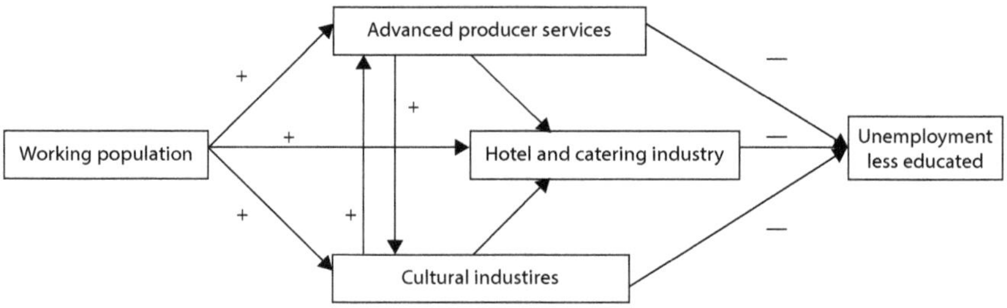

of less-educated urbanites, which was corroborated in Table 3.1 in Section 3.3. Yet, whether that effect needs to be interpreted according to the productivist logic of the polarization thesis depends on the results obtained from the testing of hypotheses 4 and 5. If the first is corroborated and the latter refuted, the low unemployment rates among the less educated in cities with high employment shares in the advanced producer services are, in the end, (partly) the result of the consumption base of cities. This is because the production base is merely a derivative of that consumption base. If, on the other hand, Hypothesis 4 needs to be refuted and Hypothesis 5 corroborated, the consumption base is (partly) derived from the production base. The interpretation in the previous section of the impact of the advanced producer services on the unemployment rates of less-educated urbanites according to polarization theory will, consequently, be sustained. The same is true for that interpretation in the case of the corroboration or refutation of both hypotheses 4 and 5. However, in the first case – with both hypotheses corroborated – the extent to which that impact can be interpreted according to the polarization thesis will, of course, depend on the extent to which the production base of cities is responsible for the clustering of advanced producer services.

The polarization thesis also predicts that the advanced producer services have an indirect, negative effect on the unemployment rates of less-educated urbanites. This is because the consumption patterns and lifestyles enabling the urban professionals they employ to work around the clock yield a high demand for low-skilled workers in the personal services and hotel and catering industries. This prediction did not, however, hold true in the analysis in the previous section, as the employment share in the hotel and catering industry did not affect the unemployment rates of less-educated urbanites in any way.

The lower right-hand side depicts the consumption-based explanation developed in this section, which predicts that the cultural industries will have a direct negative effect on the unemployment rate of less-educated urbanites (Hypothesis 6), due to a high demand for low-skilled service workers like cleaners, security staff, and servants. It is also expected that the cultural industries have an indirect negative effect on those unemployment rates, because the consumption patterns and lifestyles of the urban professionals they employ yield a high demand for low-skilled workers in the personal services and hotel and catering industries. Yet, we are already aware from the analysis in Table 3.1 that the hotel and catering industry is not responsible for varying unemployment rates across Dutch cities. Accordingly, we know that an indirect effect of the cultural industries on the unemployment rate of the less educated via the hotel and catering industry is not at play in the Dutch case.

3.5 Disentangling a productivist and consumerist explanation for unemployment among less-educated urbanites

Prior to testing hypotheses 4 to 6, I will first scrutinize the assumptions made in the previous section on the relationship between the sizes of the working population and the employment shares in the advanced producer services, cultural industries, and the hotel and catering industry. To do this, I have calculated the correlations between the variables measuring these sizes and shares, while also controlling for the nested structure of the dataset (years within cities). The findings are reported in Table 3.2, which indicates that, just as previously found on numerous occasions, the employment shares of the economic activities under study are the largest in the biggest cities. In addition, and this is in line with studies on the United States (Currid & Connolly, 2008; Florida, 2003, 2005), cities with the highest employment shares in the advanced producer services also have the highest employment shares in the cultural industries. Consequently, the impact of the former on the unemployment rates of less-educated urbanites reported in Section 3.3 may be (partly) spurious. If this is indeed the case, the latter also (partly) accounts for that impact. Strikingly, the employment share in the hotel and catering industry is positively related to that in the advanced producer services, but not to that in the cultural industries. This is in accordance with the assumptions made in the polarization thesis, but is contrary to those in the theorizing in the previous section on the role of the consumption base of cities on labour demand.

Table 3.2 Partial correlations (controlled for year) between the working population, and the employment shares in the advanced producer services, the cultural industries and the hotel and catering industry in the 22 Dutch metropolitan areas (1995-2007)

	(1)	(2)	(3)	(4)
Working population (1)	1.00	0.38***	0.20**	0.38***
Advanced producer services (2)		1.00	0.35***	0.20**
Cultural industries (3)			1.00	-0.01
Hotel and catering industry (4)				1.00
$N = 286$				

Source: StatLine CBS (own calculations)
*$p < 0.05$; **$p < 0.01$; ***$p < 0.001$

Hypotheses 4 and 5 are directed at disentangling the consumerist and productivist chains of event theorized by Florida and Sassen, respectively, which cannot be inferred by the correlations reported in Table 3.2. However, for the causal claims in those theories to be empirically valid, a necessary condition is that causes precede effects. Moreover, although causality cannot be demonstrated by a statistical analysis, this essential condition can be. The most obvious way to do this is to model time lags, as has recently been demonstrated by Neal (2012) when tackling a similar causality problem.

The first three columns in Table 3.3 test Hypothesis 4: advanced producer services settle in cities that are rich in cultural amenities. The first column shows that the variance in the producer services largely exists at the city level ((4.48 / (4.48 + 1.52)) = 74.7%); the bulk of the variance in employment in the advanced producer services can thus be attributed to city-level differences, and not differences in time. Models 1 and 2 test Hypothesis 4 by modelling a time lag of one and two years, respectively (the scores on the independent variables in the models are one and two years prior to those in the dependent variable), while also controlling for agglomeration effects. Both models show that the presence of advanced producer services strongly depends on these effects: the coefficient of the working population is positive, very strong,

Table 3.3 Share of employment in the advanced producer services and the cultural industries in the 22 Dutch metropolitan areas (1996-2007), explained by the employment shares in the cultural industries and the advanced producer services, respectively (multilevel regression analysis; entries are regression coefficients; estimation: maximum likelihood)

	Advanced producer services			Cultural industries		
	Null model	*Model 1* (t–1)	*Model 2* (t–2)	*Null model*	*Model 1* (t–1)	*Model 2* (t–2)
Independents						
Constant	21.63***	-7.79	1.10	3.84***	3.15**	3.50***
Working population		6.05***	4.16***		-0.01	-0.15
Cultural industries		0.56*	0.53*			
Advanced producer services					0.03**	0.05***
Variance metropolitan level ($N = 22$)	4.48	4.50	4.08	1.00	0.95	0.95
Variance year level	1.52	1.36	1.21	0.32	0.32	0.30
Log likelihood	-535.97	-510.02	-442.79	-127.52	-122.46	-104.84
N	264	264	242	264	264	242

Source: StatLine CBS (own calculations)
$^{*}p < 0.05$; $^{**}p < 0.01$; $^{***}p < 0.001$

and significant. In addition, there is also some indication that these services prefer to settle in cities that are rich in cultural amenities. Indeed, there is a positive relationship between employment in the cultural industries and that in the producer services one and two years later, although the effects are somewhat weak. This corroborates Hypothesis 4.

Columns four to six test Hypothesis 5: employment in the cultural industries depends on employment in the advanced producer services. The null model indicates that the bulk of the variance in employment in the cultural industries, like that in employment in the advanced producer services, exists at the city level ((1.00 / (1.00 + 0.32)) = 75.8%). Yet, unlike the advanced producer services, the cultural industries do not depend on agglomeration effects. This is a surprising finding – the cultural industries are always considered to be an outright metropolitan phenomena – and will be further discussed in the concluding sections of this chapter. The two right-hand side columns also indicate that employment in the cultural industries does depend on employment in the advanced producer services: there is a positive, significant relationship between the former and employment in the latter one or two years earlier. This corroborates Hypothesis 5.

In short, the analyses in Table 3.2 suggest that both Florida's consumerist argument and Sassen's productivist version are empirically valid: advanced producer services settle in places that are rich in cultural amenities, and these amenities become more significant in cities with a high share of the advanced producer services. It should be noted, however, that the extent to which the presence of the one determines the other is rather small. This is in line with a recent study on the Dutch case over a somewhat shorter time span (Van der Waal, 2013b), although that research did report an insignificant, positive effect of the employment share in advanced producer services on the presence of cultural industries one or two years later. As a result, it refuted the productivist logic, while corroborating the consumerist version. Yet, as an assessment over a longer period (as reported in Table 3.3) yields more reliable results, it seems safe to conclude that both forms of logic are in place in Dutch cities.

Now that we know that Sassen's productivist line of argument – labour follows capital – passes the test, it already seems safe to conclude that the effect of the employment share in the advanced producer services on the unemployment rates of less-educated urbanites found in Table 3.1 needs to be partly interpreted according to her polarization thesis. Yet, it may still be the case that, in accordance with consumerist theorizing, the cultural industries also negatively affect the unemployment rates of less-educated urbanites, as predicted by Hypothesis 6. If this is correct, it might also (partly) account for the negative effect of the advanced producer services on those unemployment rates. Identifying to what extent varying unemployment rates among the less educated in Dutch cities can be interpreted according to Sassen's polarization thesis, therefore, calls for an additional test, which will be set out in Table 3.4.

The first model in Table 3.4 reproduces the findings reported in Model 2 from Table 3.1. The question is whether the negative effect of the advanced producer services on the unemployment of less-educated urbanites found there will be accompanied by a negative effect of the cultural industries on that unemployment. The coefficient of *cultural industries* in Model 2 clearly indicates that this question needs to be answered in the negative; it is insignificant and, if it were significant, it would be positive instead of negative. This refutes Hypothesis 6. Overall, the analyses performed in this chapter indicate that the labour demand resulting from the clustering of advanced producer services in Dutch cities occurs according to the direct effect in Sassen's polarization thesis, and not on the basis of Hamnett's professionalization thesis or the consumerist theorizing developed in the previous section, which was inspired by the work of, among others, Florida, Clark, and Glaeser.

Table 3.4 Unemployment rate of the less educated in the 22 Dutch metropolitan areas (1996-2007), explained by the employment shares in the advanced producer services, the hotel and catering industry, and the cultural industries (multilevel regression analysis; entries are regression coefficients; estimation: maximum likelihood)

	Model 1	Model 2
Independents	*B*	*B*
Constant	11.50***	10.43***
Advanced producer services	-0.22***	-0.24***
Hotel and catering industry	-0.04	-0.05
Cultural industries		0.38
Controls		
Age 15-24	-0.17**	-0.17**
Variance metropolitan level (*N* = 22)	1.45	1.44
Variance year level (*N* = 12)	1.49	1.48
Log likelihood	-507.96	-506.50

Source: StatLine CBS (own calculations)
*$p < 0.05$; **$p < 0.01$; ***$p < 0.001$

3.6 Conclusions

This chapter assessed the impact of the clustering of advanced producer services on urban unemployment rates. According to the polarization thesis in the global city theoretical framework, this clustering leads to high labour demand for both highly-skilled and low-skilled service workers. The professionalization thesis, on the other hand, asserts that this clustering leads to high labour demand for highly-skilled service workers, but low demand for their low-skilled service counterparts. Consequently, according to the polarization thesis, the unemployment rate of less-educated urbanites will be the lowest in cities with the highest share of advanced producer services. Meanwhile, according to professionalization theory, it will be the highest in those cities. As it is presently unclear which one of these is correct, this chapter revolved around the following research question: *What is the impact of the clustering of advanced producer services on the unemployment rate of less-educated urbanites?*

A previous comparison of the occupational hierarchy in the global city of Amsterdam with that in Rotterdam revealed that both occupational polarization and professionalization occur in contemporary Dutch cities, albeit under different conditions (Burgers & Musterd 2002). In particular, it was found that polarization occurred in Amsterdam, while there is professionalization in Rotterdam. These authors consequently suggested that the latter thus had to cope with a mismatch between labour demand and supply at the bottom of the labour market. This suggestion is in accordance with the arguments of the polarization thesis: only urban economies with a high share of employment in the advanced producer services yield a high labour demand for both the highly and the less educated. The comparison in this chapter of the impact of the employment share in the advanced producer services on the unemployment rate of less-educated urbanites in the 22 Dutch metropolitan areas between 1996 and 2008 confirmed this argument. As could be expected on the basis of the polarization thesis, the unemployment rate is the lowest in cities with the highest share of advanced producer services. If professionalization theorizing was correct, this rate would be the highest in such cities. The answer to the central question of this chapter is, therefore, that the clustering of advanced producer services reduces the unemployment rates of less-educated urbanites, just as Sassen's polarization thesis predicts.

It must be noted, however, that the findings in this chapter only partly confirm the polarization thesis; the indirect or multiplier effect that the theory predicts due to the consumption patterns of the professionals employed in the advanced producer services was not identified. Along with the possibility that a too narrow operationalization of that indirect effect due to data limitations (relevant consumer services other than the hotel and catering industry could not be measured at the city level; compare Note 3) is responsible for this finding, two interrelated Dutch peculiarities might also account for it. Firstly, the Netherlands is a relatively generous welfare state and has a relatively strongly-regulated labour market that accompanies it. As a result, it is a context where the consumption patterns of the higher educated are least likely to boost the demand for low-skilled service workers, because the latter are less dependent on the labour market to meet their subsistence needs than those in many other developed economies. Secondly, the relatively high minimum wage levels in the Netherlands are likely to hamper the creation of many service activities in the hotel and catering and personal service sectors. If these two Dutch peculiarities are indeed the reason for the absence of the indirect labour demand due to the clustering of advanced producer services, as predicted by the polarization thesis, this would mean that in less decommodified labour markets – most notably the United Kingdom and the United States – the indirect effect predicted on the basis of the polarization thesis is more likely to kick in. It is, however, for future research to investigate whether this is correct.

A third Dutch peculiarity that might account for the unexpected finding that the hotel and catering industry does not affect the job opportunities of less-educated urbanites in the cities under scrutiny is that this industry provides students with part-time or sideline jobs, instead of full-time work for less-educated urbanites. This post-facto explanation is in line with the finding that high employment shares in the advanced producer services are accompanied by high employment shares in the hotel and catering industry (Table 3.2), as theorized in Sassen's polarization thesis. Meanwhile, those high employment shares in the hotel and catering industry do not translate into low unemployment rates among less-educated urbanites (Table 3.1). This reasoning is also in line with the empirical observation that the hotel and catering industry in the Netherlands provides popular sideline jobs for students. The advanced producer services might therefore fuel a multiplier effect due to the consumption patterns of the professionals they employ, as claimed in the polarization thesis after all, although this does not emerge from the analyses performed in this chapter due to the focus on the unemployment rate of less-educated urbanites. Further research is thus needed to examine whether this is actually the case.

After addressing the polarization versus professionalization dispute in the global city debate, this chapter confronted the empirical corroboration of the former thesis with more recent theorizing in urban studies that is based on radically different arguments. The consumerist theorizing on urban economic development by Richard Florida fundamentally alters the productivist assumptions in Sassen's polarization thesis. The reason for doing so is that 'studies of the city traditionally posit a division between a city's economy and its culture, with culture subordinate in explanatory power to "work"' (Clark et al., 2003: 291). In contrast, Florida, Clark, and others claim that it can just as easily be the other way around: the settlement of firms is determined by the cultural amenities in cities, as the latter attract the professionals that the former are searching for. Moreover, the expectation deduced from this line of argument, i.e. that advanced producer service firms settle in places that are rich in cultural amenities, was confirmed. Although this confirmation is in line with Florida's most radical claims, it did not invalidate polarization theory's interpretation of the impact of the advanced producer services on the unemployment rates of less-educated urbanites in Dutch cities. This is for three reasons: 1) the settlement of the advanced producer services is largely determined by factors other than the cultural industries; 2) in line with productivist reasoning, the advanced producer services also determine the prominence of cultural industries, albeit minimally so; and 3) the cultural industries do not negatively affect the unemployment rates among the less educated across Dutch cities, while the advanced producer services do so substantially. A possible explanation for the limited effects addressed under the first two points is that the clustering of cultural industries and/or advanced producer services is – in the case of the latter, in addition to being the result of agglomeration effects – mainly driven by a clustering (Porter, 1998) and/or network (Grabher & Powell, 2004) logic. This is, however, for future research to decide.

Two other remarkable findings also call for post-facto hypothesizing. The first of these is that agglomeration effects did not account for the settlement of cultural industries in Dutch cities. An explanation might be provided by the previously mentioned extended welfare state in the Netherlands. Subsidies for cultural activities also make these less dependent on large publics than when they are exposed to market forces. They are, therefore, much easier to maintain in smaller cities than is the case in less regulated countries. The final, unexpected, finding related to consumerist theorizing that calls for future clarification is the fact that in cities with high shares of employment in the cultural industries, unemployment rates are no lower than in cities with low shares of this type of employment. The reason for this unexpected pattern may lie in the small size of the Netherlands. The production and consumption of cultural amenities in cities other than the ones where their producers and consumers live and/or work is therefore an option that is mainly absent in larger developed economies. As a result, the potential job openings that cultural production and consumption provide for less-educated workers might be less place-bound in the Netherlands than consumption-based theories of urban development maintain. Consequently, local unemployment rates and local employment in the cultural industries do not necessarily need to be empirically related in the Dutch case. All the interpretations of unexpected findings in this paragraph imply that in bigger and less-regulated advanced economies – most notably the United States – the presence of cultural amenities can go hand in hand with a high demand for low-skilled service workers. Future research needs to decide whether this is correct, or whether the theorizing on this matter in this chapter is simply empirically invalid.

After discussing the findings of this chapter in relation to the theories that guided the analyses – polarization, professionalization, and the consumerist alternative to the first of these – it is now time to relate these to the global city debate at large.

Firstly, previous comparisons of cities in the former Federal Republic of Germany and the United States (Kasarda, 1985; Kasarda & Friedrichs, 1985, 1986) did yield results that strongly resonate with the findings in this book. In particular, these authors demonstrated that cities with a low share of employment in the advanced producer services generate the fewest labour market opportunities for the less educated. As the study of Kasarda and Friedrichs used data from the 1970s and early 1980s, it concluded that 'we actually do not know whether the high unemployment rates currently confronting many Western economies are a relatively permanent structural feature or simply reflect temporarily incomplete adaptation; if the latter (...) substantial new service sector jobs (both high and low skill) will be created in the long run, relieving the mismatch' (1986: 22). Yet, the analyses in this chapter on data from the mid-1990s to 2008 suggest that the mismatch between labour demand and supply induced by the 1980s' deindustrialization of cities in the advanced economies is *neither* a permanent feature *nor* a temporarily incomplete adaptation. Instead, both occurred; it was a temporary feature in cities with a high share of employment in advanced producer services, while in those with a low share of these services it seems to be permanent (cf. Pratschke & Morlicchio, 2012). The latter thus still have to cope with a mismatch between labour demand and supply. What the future brings for cities with a low employment share in the advanced producer services is unclear, but in past decades this mismatch has proved to be persistent. In addition, and more importantly, the previous chapter indicated that the driving force that could alleviate this problem – the clustering of advanced producer services – is least developed in those cities.

Secondly, this is the first study in the global city debate to model both the direct and indirect effects of the polarization thesis. That merely the former effect was corroborated, while all the available evidence indicates that the labour market of the global city of Amsterdam is polarized, helps in interpreting results from earlier studies. After finding polarization in Amsterdam and professionalization in Rotterdam, Burgers and Musterd (2002) hypothesized that the reason for that difference is the consumption pattern of the professionals employed in the advanced producer services, as Amsterdam has a higher share of these workers than Rotterdam. In short, they propose that the indirect effect must be responsible for the difference between the two cities. Yet, the current study indicates that, by now, the direct effect in the polarization thesis is enough for polarization to occur. This suggests that the findings of previous studies that found professionalization with respect to occupational change in cities can also be interpreted on the basis of the arguments of the polarization thesis. Earlier studies on Amsterdam (Hamnett, 1994a), London (Hamnett, 1994b, 1996a, 2004), and Paris (Rhein, 1996) used data from the 1980s. Back then, the employment share in the advanced producer services might have been too small to yield enough labour demand for less-educated service workers. The fact that Hamnett found professionalization of the occupational hierarchy in Amsterdam in the 1980s, while Burgers and Musterd found polarization of this same hierarchy in the city in the 1990s, also points in this direction. This, then, suggests that the occupational structure of London, Paris, and other European global cities is polarized by now, although this has not yet been documented: there are simply no studies on these cities that use data from that period. By using a method other than the one applied in this chapter, a study by May et al. (2007) on London also strongly points in that direction.

Thirdly, just like the findings in Chapter 2, those in this chapter indicate that the widely-held assumption in the global city debate that global cities such as New York and Amsterdam wear the future guise of cities lower down the urban hierarchy (e.g. Burgers, 1996; Mollenkopf, 2009; Mollenkopf & Castells, 1992; Vaattovaara & Kortteinen, 2003) is problematic. There are two reasons why this is the case. In the first place, the previous chapter demonstrated that the economic base of all cities does not become similar to that of the global city of Amsterdam. On the contrary, the employment share in the advanced producer services increased much more in Amsterdam, and in the most service-oriented cities in general, than in former industrial strongholds, just as argued in the global city theoretical framework. The findings in this chapter thus revealed that the former cities yield much more labour demand for less-educated urbanites than the latter, which consequently have to cope with a mismatch between labour demand and supply.

The second reason why the widely-held assumption that global cities wear the future guise of cities lower down the urban hierarchy is problematic is because it comes down to assuming that the occupational hierarchy of all cities will polarize (polarization thesis) or professionalize (professionalization thesis). Yet, all the available evidence suggests that the occupational hierarchy of *all* cities will *neither* polarize *nor* professionalize. Instead, the findings in Chapter 2, combined with those in this chapter, imply that there will be both polarization and professionalization of the occupational hierarchy of cities in the advanced economies, albeit under different conditions. In cities with the highest share of employment in the advanced producer services, the occupational hierarchy is likely to be polarized, especially given the previous chapter's demonstration that this employment share increased most strongly in these cities. On the other hand, in cities with a low share of employment in the advanced producer services, the occupational hierarchy is likely to be professionalized, particularly because, as reported in the previous chapter, this employment share barely increases at all in those cities.

4 Foreign direct investment and immigration

Displacing the locus of explanation away from poverty or economic stagnation in sending countries and onto the processes that link sending and receiving country introduces a set of variables into the analysis not usually thought of as pertaining to immigration. Such linkages are constituted through processes that are historically specific. In the current period, the internationalization of production is central in the constitution of such linkages (*Sassen, 1988: 9-10*).

4.1 Introduction

This chapter aims to assess the central claims in the global city theoretical framework on what drives immigration flows from newly-industrializing countries to cities in the advanced economies in general, and to global cities in particular. It is argued in this framework that the classic migration theories, which revolve around underdevelopment and population pressures, fall short in explaining these immigrant flows. Indeed, these flows should instead be understood as being driven by a combination of a *new* push and a *new* pull factor. The former concerns foreign direct investment from the advanced economies in newly-industrializing countries, while the latter relates to the massive labour demand for low-skilled service workers driven by the clustering of advanced producer services in cities.

Section 4.2 will further elaborate on these claims and how they relate to classic explanations of immigration from less-developed to advanced economies. Subsequently, Section 4.3 will examine their empirical validity. The findings of this assessment will be discussed in the concluding section, 4.4, which will answer the following research questions: *Can the new immigration to cities in the advanced economies be explained by foreign direct investments?* (Research Question 4), and: *Does the clustering of advanced producer services attract immigrant labour from newly-industrializing countries?* (Research Question 5).

4.2 Immigration in the global city: theoretical framework

Before Sassen published *The Global City* in 1991, her scholarly interest primarily concerned immigration flows from newly-industrializing countries to large cities in the advanced economies. In fact, the roots of the global city theoretical framework can be found in her studies on that subject, as is clearly revealed by titles like *The New Labour Demand in Global Cities* (Sassen-Koob, 1984b) and *New York City: Economic Restructuring and Immigration* (Sassen-Koob, 1986). In her theory on immigration from newly-industrializing countries to large cities in the advanced economies, Sassen combined the push and pull factors of immigration with the argument that 'the same set of basic processes that (...) promoted emigration from several rapidly industrializing countries (...) also promoted immigration into several booming global cities' (1988: 22). This 'set of basic processes' is the new international division of labour caused by the outsourcing of parts of the production process from the advanced economies to newly-industrializing countries, which is often abstractly referred to as foreign direct investments, or FDI.

The pull factor in this theoretical framework has been extensively elaborated on in the previous chapter: there is a high labour demand for low-skilled service workers due to the clustering of advanced producer services. It is argued that this clustering 'generates low wage jobs directly, through the structure of the work process, and indirectly, through the structure of the high income life-styles of those therein employed' (Sassen-Koob, 1986: 99; cf. Sassen-Koob, 1984a, 1984b, 1985; Sassen, 1988, 2001, 2006a, 2012). The direct labour demand is for cleaners, clerks, security, and the like (Sassen, 2000: 142, 2006a: 197, 2012), while the indirect demand concerns 'an army of low-wage workers' (Sassen-Koob, 1985: 262; cf. Sassen-Koob, 1984a, 1984b, 1986; Sassen, 1988, 2001, 2006a, 2012) in the consumer services to cater to the professionals employed in the advanced producer services. It also refers to workers in a downgraded manufacturing sector directed at limited runs of customized production, as well as employees in small specialist retail outlets offering limited edition consumer goods (Sassen-Koob, 1984b, 1986; Sassen, 1993). In short, '[t]he expansion in the supply of low-wage jobs generated by major growth sectors is one of the key factors in the continuation at ever-higher levels of the current immigration' (Sassen-Koob, 1988: 146).

The push factor of immigration in this theoretical framework is induced by the outsourcing by multinationals of parts of the production process to newly-industrializing countries. These foreign direct investments mostly concern production sites for labour-intensive manufacturing and service activities. According to Sassen, such investment flows encourage immigration flows in the opposite direction: from newly-industrializing countries to cities, especially global cities, in the advanced economies.

The central argument explaining how this comes about is put forward in detail in *Direct Foreign Investment: A Migration Push-Factor?* (Sassen-Koob, 1984a) and *The Mobility of Labor and Capital: A Study in International Investment and Labor Flow* (1988). The underlying mechanism is aptly summarized by the title of the subsection in the latter: *The Growth of Direct Foreign Investment and the Uprooting of People* (1988: 17). This argues that investments in newly-industrializing countries cause the 'disruption of traditional work structures' due to 'the transformation of subsistence workers into wage-labor' (Sassen, 1988: 18). As a consequence, 'this "new industrialisation" has generated domestic and international migrations within the regions which eventually may overflow into long-distance migration' (Sassen, 1988: 18). That this long-distance migration is primarily directed to the advanced economies, especially to those from where the investments came, is because:

> the presence of such investments creates cultural-ideological and objective links with the countries providing this capital (...) Besides the long recognized westernization effect of large-scale foreign investment in the less developed world, there is the more specific impact on workers employed in production for export or in the services in the export sector. These workers are using their labor power in the production of goods and services demanded by people and firms in the U.S. or any other highly developed country. *The distance between a job in the off-shore plant or office and in the on-shore plant is subjectively reduced.* Under these conditions emigration may begin to emerge as an option actually felt by individuals. (Sassen, 1988: 18-9, italics added)

According to the global city theoretical framework, then, the same process that leads to the clustering of advanced producer services in global cities leads to immigration from newly-industrializing countries to those cities: investment in newly-industrializing countries and the new international division of labour that stems from it. The disruption of the traditional work structures in newly-industrializing countries because of these investments stimulates immigration to the advanced economies in general, but especially to global cities due to the high labour demand for low-skilled services. Furthermore, the cultural-ideological and objective links between the sending and receiving countries that result from foreign direct investments often direct these immigration flows in the opposite direction of the investment flows. Put differently, these immigration flows are primarily directed at the advanced economy that invested in the country from which this immigration stems.

With this line of reasoning, Sassen is *not* claiming that theories on 'classical' push factors of immigration from underdeveloped countries to the advanced economies, such as economic stagnation, overpopulation, political turmoil, and poverty, are wrong. Furthermore, that the direction of those immigrant flows is influenced by political ties like previous colonial bonds, military exercises, and immigration legislation is not denied. What is, however, claimed is that these explanations fall short in explaining the *new* immigrant flows induced by the current phase of economic globalization; and can instead be understood according to the theoretical reasoning addressed above.

As such, Sassen's argument aims to explain *recent* immigration flows from newly-industrializing countries to the advanced economies, especially to global cities. In her publications on this subject, Sassen therefore labels these migration flows as 'the new immigration phase' (Sassen-Koob, 1984b: 158), 'the current phase of (...) migration' (Sassen-Koob, 1986: 86), or 'the current migration phase' (Sassen, 1988: 4). To explain these flows, Sassen considers *foreign investment to be a neglected variable*, as indicated by the title of the first chapter in *The Mobility of Labor and Capital: A Study in International Investment and Labor Flow* (1988: 12). The fact that it was published almost 20 years later in abbreviated form under the same heading as a chapter in *The Migration Reader: Exploring Politics and Policy* (2006b) reveals that Sassen still considers foreign direct investments to be an under-assessed explanation for current immigration from less-developed economies to cities in the advanced economies in general, and to global cities in particular.

This under-assessment is no overstatement, as the number of empirical studies on the impact of foreign direct investments on immigration from underdeveloped to the advanced economies is rather limited. As early as 1987, Ricketts found that these investments drive immigration from countries in the Caribbean region to the United States, while eleven years later Yang found that 'foreign investment abroad is a push factor for migration' (1998: 378) to the US, as did Aroca and Maloney (2005), by assessing investments from the United States in Mexico. More recently, Sanderson and Kentor (2008) found that out-migration from 25 less-developed countries was indeed driven by increased foreign investments. Yet, two other studies produced different results: Hayase (2001) demonstrated that investments from Japan in East Asian economies can also hamper out-migration due to the resulting economic development, and the most recent study by Wang et al. (2013) on the impact of investments from OECD countries in economically less-developed nations reported quite similar findings.

As well as yielding scattered results, these six studies concern state-level inquiries, three on migration to the United States, one on migration to Japan, and two on out-migration from less-developed economies. They thus all assessed migration between nations instead of from less-developed economies to cities in the advanced economies with a high labour demand for low-skilled service workers. As a consequence, the question of whether the new immigration to cities in the advanced economies is driven by a combination of push and pull factors spurred by foreign direct investments, as argued by Sassen, is still unanswered. This chapter therefore aims to provide a response to this question by assessing whether the growth of new immigrant groups in Dutch cities can indeed be explained by Dutch foreign investments in the countries from where these immigrants originate. If the answer is 'yes', the expectation would be that *the growth of new immigrant groups in Dutch cities is greatest from the countries where Dutch foreign direct investments increased the most* (Hypothesis 1).

After assessing this push factor of the new immigration, I will examine the pull factor outlined in the theoretical framework above and in Chapter 3. It is argued that the labour demand for low-skilled service workers that is directly and indirectly induced by the clustering of advanced producer services pulls immigrants from newly-industrializing economies to cities in the advanced economies. If this is correct, it can be expected that *the growth of new immigrant groups is strongest in cities with the greatest employment growth in both the advanced producer services* (Hypothesis 2) *and the hotel and catering industry* (Hypothesis 3).[7]

4.3 Assessing the push and pull factors of the new immigration

4.3.1 Assessing Dutch FDI as a push factor for immigration

Contrary to the previous chapter's analyses, the push factor analyses in this section do not compare cities, but instead contrast the growth of immigrant groups within cities (see Appendix B for a detailed description of the data used and the precise operationalization of the variables). These groups are defined by the countries from where the immigrants originate, and 22 of

7 See Note 3 on the data limitations for operationalizing the indirect labour-demand effect.

Table 4.1 Zero-order correlations between the variables used for testing the FDI-migration nexus and classical migration theories ($N = 19$)

	(1)	(2)	(3)	(4)	(5)	(6)	(7)	(8)	(9)	(10)
Growth immigrants Amsterdam (1)	1.00	0.83**	0.47*	0.23	-0.18	-0.18	-0.36	0.23	0.12	-0.16
Growth immigrants Dutch cities (2)		1.00	0.37	0.14	-0.14	-0.13	-0.33	0.56*	-0.11	-0.24
Dutch FDI (3)			1.00	0.72**	0.43~	-0.62**	0.17	-0.23	-0.03	-0.19
Total FDI (4)				1.00	0.60**	-0.77**	0.25	-0.53*	0.21	0.03
GDP per capita (5)					1.00	-0.50*	0.17	-0.32	0.23	0.22
Population growth (6)						1.00	-0.13	0.48*	0.07	-0.11
Distance (7)							1.00	-0.28	-0.44~	-0.49*
Asylum requests (8)								1.00	-0.25	-0.12
Migrant stock Amsterdam (9)									1.00	0.76**
Migrant stock Dutch cities (10)										1.00

Source: OECD, World Bank, UNCTAD, *IND*, and *CBS* (own calculations)
~$p < 0.10$; *$p < 0.05$; **$p < 0.01$

these immigrant-sending countries could be distinguished by the available data sources (see Table B2 in Appendix B). It was possible to use nineteen of these immigrant-sending countries for the analyses below, and these assessments will consequently be performed on nineteen immigrant groups. The analyses will relate the growth of those immigrant groups in Dutch cities to the growth in Dutch FDI in the corresponding immigrant-sending nations, while also controlling for the characteristics of those countries which, according to classic migration theories, inspire out-migration to advanced economies. This procedure will be conducted for the global city of Amsterdam, and for the 22 metropolitan areas combined.

As a preliminary test of the FDI-immigration nexus and the competing classic migration theories, I have calculated the bivariate relationship for all variables used in the regression analyses to test Hypothesis 1. Table 4.1 reports the results. Along with some obvious strong correlations, i.e. between 1) growth in immigrants to Amsterdam and growth in immigrants to Dutch cities, 2) immigrants in 1996 in Amsterdam and immigrants in 1996 in Dutch cities, and 3) Dutch FDI and total FDI, some other relationships are quite informative.[8]

Firstly, the variable of *asylum requests* is strongly correlated to *growth in immigrants to Dutch cities*, but not to *growth in immigrants to Amsterdam*. This mirrors Dutch migration policies, as housing arranged for asylum seekers is scattered across the country. Furthermore, as the number of asylum requests can be regarded as a measure of political turmoil, the strongly negative correlation with *total FDI* is not a surprise: political instability hampers the influx of foreign investments. Secondly, the bivariate relationships between both measures of *immigrant growth* and *Dutch FDI* are positive, as could be expected on the basis of the FDI-migration nexus. Yet, in the end, the litmus test for the empirical validity of that nexus cannot be based on a bivariate relationship, but instead needs to control for other explanations, and will be performed in the regression analyses in Tables 4.2 (migration to Amsterdam) and 4.3 (migration to 22 metropolitan areas combined).[9] In the first model, it is

8 As the regression analyses in Chapter 4 are based on small samples, I will use a less strict criterion to determine whether a relationship is significant or not (a p value below 0.1 instead of one below 0.05 will suffice).

9 In Chapter 3, the regression coefficients of the variables that were relevant for testing the hypotheses were much easier to interpret than those of the variables in Tables 4.2 and 4.3. The reason for this is that the former are based on variables that indicate percentages (employment shares of industries, unemployment rates), while those in Chapter 4 are based on variables that measure units in a logarithmic form (see Appendix B). Nevertheless, the coefficients in Tables

demonstrated that the coefficients of two out of three control variables are in the expected direction: the highest immigrant growth stems from countries that are close by, and a high number of asylum requests is accompanied by high immigrant growth.[10] To control for the migration flows stimulated by immigrants who are already settled – so-called 'chain migration' (Portes, 2000) – the number of immigrants in 1996 is also modelled. However, unlike what might be expected on the basis of arguments centering on chain migration, this factor is not positively related to immigrant growth.

Model 1 in Tables 4.2 and 4.3 also contains the indicator for the total FDI in the immigrant-sending countries, which yields a fairly strongly positive, significant coefficient: a high level of investment in immigrant-sending countries is accompanied by a high immigrant influx from those countries to both Amsterdam and the 22 Dutch metropolitan areas combined. This suggests a general westernization effect of FDI, as has previously been emphasized by scholars such as Sassen (1988) and Massey (1988). However, our primary interest in this chapter is whether Dutch FDI spawns immigration to the Netherlands. Accordingly, *growth Dutch FDI* is entered into Model 2 of both Table 4.2 and Table 4.3.

In the table containing the analysis on migration flows to Amsterdam, the positive impact of Dutch FDI on those flows is strong. What is more, the effect of total FDI is completely explained away after entering *growth Dutch FDI*. This indicates that the influx of immigrants into Amsterdam – at least from 1996 onwards – is partly driven by the cultural links that stem from Dutch FDI in their countries of origin, and not by an all-encompassing westernization effect that accompanies FDI in general. For the immigrant flows into the 22 Dutch metropolitan areas combined, this seems to be less clear. Although there is a positive effect of Dutch FDI that partly accounts for the impact of total FDI, it is less convincing than in the case of Amsterdam.

Given the small number of immigrant groups in the dataset, all variables that have thus far proved to be irrelevant have been removed from Model 3. For the analysis on Amsterdam (Table 4.2), this means that *growth total FDI*

4.2 and 4.3 still report whether independent variables will significantly relate to the dependent variable, and, if so, in what direction. In other words, those coefficients still indicate, at a glance, whether hypotheses are corroborated or rejected.

10 As the hypotheses do predict the direction of a relationship, one-sided tests will be used to determine whether they are false. Such tests will be applied to all the hypotheses in this study if there are no counter-hypotheses predicting an inverse direction of the relationship in question.

Table 4.2 Growth immigrant groups in Amsterdam (1996-2009) explained by the growth in (Dutch) foreign direct investments, population growth, and GDP per capita (regression analysis; entries are regression coefficients; estimation: ordinary least squares)

	Model 1	Model 2	Model 3	Model 4	
Independents	*B*	*B*	*B*	*B*	*VIF*
Constant	54.42	-2467.29	-2437.92*	-1563.42	
Growth total FDI	158.60*	29.89	_	_	
Growth Dutch FDI		440.55~	495.35**	573.80**	1.73
Population growth				-74.04	2.16
GDP per capita				-195.59*	1.41
Controls					
Distance	-0.11~	-0.10~	-0.10*	-0.09*	1.12
Asylum requests	0.01~	0.01	0.01	0.01	1.43
Immigrants 1996	-45.05	15.98	_	_	
R^2	0.36	0.48	0.47	0.58	
N	19	19	19	19	

Source: OECD, World Bank, UNCTAD, *IND*, and *CBS* (own calculations)
$\sim p < 0.10$; $^{*}p < 0.05$; $^{**}p < 0.01$, one-sided

Table 4.3 Growth immigrant groups in the 22 Dutch metropolitan areas combined (1996-2009) explained by the growth in (Dutch) foreign direct investments, population growth, and GDP per capita (regression analysis; entries are regression coefficients; estimation: ordinary least squares)

	Model 1	Model 2	Model 3	Model 4	
Independents	*B*	*B*	*B*	*B*	*VIF*
Constant	9365.24	2585.26	-12424.54*	-8985.73	
Growth total FDI	997.65**	723.39*	589.85~	910.98*	3.52
Growth Dutch FDI		985.97	1494.19~	1488.40~	2.23
Population growth				_	
GDP per capita				-945.86*	1.58
Controls					
Distance	-0.66*	-0.62*	-0.37~	-0.36~	1.10
Asylum requests	0.14**	0.14**	0.16**	0.16**	1.55
Immigrants 1996	-1489.50	-1265.52	_	_	
R^2	0.63	0.73	0.68	0.75	
N	19	19	19	19	

Source: OECD, World Bank, UNCTAD, *IND*, and *CBS* (own calculations)
$\sim p < 0.10$; $^{*}p < 0.05$; $^{**}p < 0.01$, one-sided

and *immigrants 1996* have has been removed, while for the analysis on the 22 metropolitan areas combined only the latter variable has been excluded. For Amsterdam, this does not alter the findings thus far, while for the 22 agglomerations combined the effect of Dutch FDI increases in strength and that of total FDI decreases. Immigration to Amsterdam, then, seems to be driven by Dutch FDI, while that to the 22 Dutch metropolitan areas combined appears to be driven by both forms of FDI. This suggests that the latter type of immigration is the result of both a general westernization effect and cultural ties stemming from Dutch FDI, while the former is merely due to Dutch cultural ties accompanying Dutch FDI. To validate these findings, they need to at least be confronted with the most dominant theories on migration from less-developed economies to developed ones, i.e. classic migration theories that focus on population pressures and underdevelopment.

The final step in the analyses on the push factor explanation presented in Model 4 in Tables 4.2 and 4.3 thus adds the indicators for the classic migration theories: *population growth* and/or *GDP per capita*. These have both been entered into Table 4.2, while only the latter has been included in Table 4.3. This is because the latter table contains one more variable, while minimizing the number of variables seems to be appropriate due to the small number of immigrant groups in the dataset. It should be noted, however, that including *population growth* in Table 4.3 does not alter the presented findings.[11] The analyses on both Amsterdam and the 22 Dutch metropolitan areas combined demonstrate that both Sassen's FDI-migration nexus and the classic migration theories can explain the increase in the number of immigrants. Not only is the impact of Dutch FDI maintained when confronted with indicators for classic migration theories, but the latter theses also have explanatory value: a low GDP per capita in immigrant-sending countries results in a major increase in immigrant numbers in both Amsterdam and the 22 Dutch metropolitan areas combined. The final model in the two tables also includes the variance inflation factors (VIF), which are all well below a score of 10. This means that, despite the sometimes high correlation between the independent variables (see Table 4.1), there is no major multicollinearity (Myers, 1990). Overall, it therefore seems to be safe to conclude that Hypothesis 1 – *The growth of immigrant populations in Dutch cities is strongest from countries where Dutch foreign direct investments increased most* – is corroborated.

11 The analyses are not reported, but are available upon request.

4.3.2 Assessing growth in the advanced producer services as a pull factor for immigration

After assessing the push factor of new immigration, it is now time to examine its alleged pull factor: the clustering of advanced producer services. As shown in the previous chapter, the Dutch cities with the highest share of employment in these services have the lowest unemployment rates among their less-educated citizens. This is in accordance with the argument of the polarization thesis, and means that the mismatch between labour demand and supply is highest in cities with the lowest share of employment in the advanced producer services. If the pull factor explanation in the FDI-migration nexus formulated by Sassen is correct, the expectation is that the rise in the number of immigrants increased the most in Dutch cities where employment in the advanced producer services also increased the most (Hypothesis 2). Furthermore, on the basis of the same explanation, it may be expected that this will partly be driven by the increase in employment in the hotel and catering industry, which is a sector that is claimed to cater to the professionals employed in the advanced producer services (Hypothesis 3).

These hypotheses will be tested in Table 4.4 with a regression analysis that relates growth in industries to the rise in total immigrant shares in the 22 Dutch metropolitan areas. Contrary to the analyses in the previous subsection, we are now comparing cities instead of immigrant groups within cities (see Appendix B for detailed information on the data used and the precise operationalization of the variables). The first model of Table 4.4 assesses the impact of the employment growth in the advanced producer services on the growth in the immigrant share in the working population in the 22 Dutch metropolitan areas. The second model examines whether the hypothesized effect of those services can (partly) be accounted for by employment in the hotel and catering industry, as suggested in Sassen's pull factor explanation. Just like the analysis on the push factor explanation, this assessment will also control for chain migration. This is because, as suggested by Sassen (Sassen-Koob, 1984b, 1986; Sassen, 1993), immigrant settlement might also result from ethnic ties and networks (cf. Portes, 2000) and the demand for immigrant labour driven by immigrants who are already settled.

Contrary to her push factor explanation, Sassen's pull factor explanation for immigrant flows from developing countries to cities in the developed economies does not yield any empirical support for the Dutch case. A rise in immigrant numbers is not significantly related to the

Table 4.4 Growth immigrant share in the working population in the 22 Dutch metropolitan areas (1997-2007) explained by the growth in the employment shares of the advanced producer services and the hotel and catering industry (1995-2007) (regression analysis; entries are regression coefficients; estimation: ordinary least squares)

	Model 1	**Model 2**	
Independents	*B*	*B*	*VIF*
Constant	0.01**	0.01*	
Growth employment advanced producer services	0.00	-0.00	1.18
Growth employment hotel and catering industry		0.29	1.08
Controls			
Immigrant stock 1997	0.22**	0.22***	1.28
R^2	0.36	0.39	
N	22	22	

Source: *CBS* (own calculations)
~$p < 0.10$; *$p < 0.05$; **$p < 0.01$, one-sided

growth in employment in the advanced producer services. If it were, employment growth in the hotel and catering industry would also not account for it, as the two types of growth yield insignificant coefficients. As a result, both hypotheses 2 and 3, which were deduced from the pull factor explanation, must be rejected. The pull factor rationale in Sassen's FDI-migration nexus cannot therefore account for the settlement of immigrants in Dutch cities, which, consequently, clearly calls for another explanation.

Chain migration seems to be an appropriate alternative explanation, as the indicator for it in this analysis has a quite strongly positive effect on immigrant growth. It must be noted, however, that it is a rather crude indicator, as it does not discriminate between immigrant-sending countries. In the Netherlands, then, immigrants settle in cities where many immigrants already reside, and this is clearly not because such cities have an abundance of labour-market opportunities that are directly or indirectly driven by employment growth in the advanced producer services, as was theorized by Sassen. How the chain migration precisely comes about is, however, another research question and goes beyond the scope of this study. The concluding section will, nevertheless, further elaborate on these findings.

4.4 Conclusions

This chapter assessed the central claims in Sassen's FDI-migration nexus for immigration from less-developed economies to Dutch cities. This nexus combines a push factor explanation, which revolves around investment flows, with a pull factor version, which concerns demand for low-skilled service workers due to the clustering of advanced producer services in cities. Sassen combined these factors into one framework on the basis of the notion that they share a root cause: the new international division of labour due to the (re)location of parts of the production process from developed economies to newly-industrializing ones.

The analyses indicate that the claim concerning the push factor for migration from developing economies to developed ones is correct when applied to Dutch cities. Controlled for 1) factors which, according to classic migration theories, drive such immigration, i.e. underdevelopment and population pressures, and 2) a wide-ranging westernization effect that allegedly accompanies FDI influxes in general, Dutch investments in less-developed economies were revealed to increase migration flows from those countries to Dutch cities between 1996 and 2010. Research Question 4 of this study – *Can the new immigration to cities in the advanced economies be explained by foreign direct investments?* – can therefore be answered in the positive.

Although the findings in this chapter are in line with Sassen's push factor argument, more research is needed to uncover its empirical validity. This is firstly because the central mechanism of this explanation revolves around the uprooting of people due to the introduction of the capitalistic logic of wage labour. This study is unable to validate such a claim, as it calls for ethnographic research in the export processing zones of immigrant-sending countries.

The second, and probably most substantial, reason as to why future research could shed more light on the validity of Sassen's push factor explanation, is that the findings in this study can also be interpreted according to another theory, which essentially claims that outward FDI flows are *initiated* by immigrants, instead of the other way round (Javorcik, 2011; Kugler & Rapoport, 2007; Leblang, 2010). In this line of reasoning, it is the information that immigrants have about investment opportunities in their country of origin that drives these investment flows. As a consequence, it might be expected that it refers to highly-educated immigrants. Given that this study had to rely on a proxy to select less-educated immigrants (see Appendix B), future research on the causal direction of the relationship between FDI and immigration that was found in this study, therefore, becomes even more relevant. Nevertheless, as foreign direct investments were measured three years prior to migration flows in this research, it seems very unlikely that the results actually measure the investment flows initiated by knowledge of investment opportunities in their country of birth among immigrants in Dutch cities.

Although more research is needed to uncover the empirical validity of the push factor argument in Sassen's FDI-migration nexus, the findings in this chapter are in accordance with it, and therefore raise serious questions about policy arguments derived from the 'root causes' (Martin, 1995: 820) of immigration from less-developed economies to the advanced ones, e.g. underdevelopment, 'low wages and few jobs' (ibid.). In line with these causes, it is claimed that 'immigration countries can influence the propensity to emigrate from other countries through three major economic channels – trade, investment, aid' (ibid.). Although investments in less-developed economies do indeed lead to economic growth (Hahm & Heo, 2008), this chapter indicates that such growth does not have unequivocal consequences when it comes to migration pressures. As far as economic growth is driven by foreign direct investments, it is likely to lead to falling emigration due to improving economic conditions on the one hand, while, on the other, it strengthens or even initiates emigration due to the cultural and objective links with countries from where such investments originate (cf. Hayase, 2001; Wang et al., 2013). This 'development paradox' does, however, need to be interpreted with care, as the corroboration of the 'FDI drives emigration argument' in this study is based on investments from one advanced economy in a limited number of less-developed economies. On the other hand, one needs to keep in mind that four of the six earlier studies on the impact of FDI on migration also corroborate this link at the country level. Nevertheless, future research could shed more light on the consequences of the development paradox uncovered here when it comes to migration from less-developed economies to advanced ones.

Contrary to the push factor explanation, the pull factor explanation in Sassen's FDI-migration nexus could not be empirically corroborated here. The previous chapter and various other studies do indeed indicate that Dutch cities with a high employment share in the advanced producer services have the smallest mismatch between labour demand and supply at the bottom of the labour market. Yet, the high labour demand in those cities does not prove to be a pull factor for the new immigration: growth in the immigrant population in Dutch cities was neither related to employment growth in the advanced producer services, nor to a rise in employment in the sector that allegedly caters to the lifestyles of the professionals employed in those services. Even if the latter growth was related to a rise in immigrant numbers, this would not be in accordance with the theoretical rationale of Sassen's pull factor explanation, as it predicts that this relationship (partly) needs to account for the effect of the growth in advanced producer services. There is, however, no effect of the growth in those services on immigrant growth in the first place. This indicates that the data limitations for modelling the labour demand driven by the consumption patterns of the professionals employed in the advanced producer services reported earlier (see Note 3), cannot be responsible for the finding that the rise in immigrants in Dutch cities is not in accordance with Sassen's pull factor explanation. Accordingly, the fifth research question – *Does the clustering of advanced producer services attract immigrant labour from newly-industrializing countries?* – needs to be answered in the negative.

What might account for this finding is the factor that has been extensively discussed in the conclusions of the previous chapter: the Dutch welfare state might inhibit the creation of the 'service proletariat' demanded by the work procedures and consumption patterns of the upper occupational strata, as the relatively high wages at the bottom end of the labour market hamper the local commodification of these activities. Another possibility, which was also discussed in the concluding section of the previous chapter, is that the hotel and catering industry in the cities under study most notably provide students with part-time or sideline jobs, instead of employing less-educated urbanites, be they immigrant or native, in day jobs. In that case, the hotel and catering industry does provide potential job openings for less-educated immigrants, as theorized in the pull factor explanation in Sassen's FDI-migration nexus, but employers, for whatever reason, opt for students instead of immigrants. Future research might discover whether this post-facto explanation has empirical merit.

In addition, kinship, or ethnic or social ties with former waves of immigrants, might influence where immigrants decide to live (cf. Zorlu & Mulder, 2008), irrespective of whether this improves their labour-market position or not. Indeed, the major impact of the indicator for chain migration in the pull factor analysis strongly points in that direction. However, part of this 'chain migration' might, in the end, be related to labour demand by means of mechanisms other than the pull factor explanation assessed in this chapter. Firstly, the presence of immigrant communities might in itself lead to labour demand in the industries that cater to these communities, thus attracting new waves of immigrants (Sassen-Koob, 1984b, 1986; Sassen, 1993). If this is correct, (part of) the substantial effect of the indicator for chain migration in the pull factor analysis ultimately needs to be interpreted according to labour market logic. Secondly, the data used in this chapter do not allow the issue of whether labour demand in the informal economy attracts new waves of immigrants to be uncovered. Yet, if such an informal economy is directed at serving the consumption pattern of the professionals employed in the advanced producer services, as theorized by Sassen (Sassen-Koob, 1984b, 1986; Sassen, 1993), one would expect an effect of the growth in advanced producer services in the analysis of the pull factor explanation. That the growth in those services had no impact on immigrant growth is therefore at odds with this theorizing.

All that being said, this study is the first attempt to assess Sassen's FDI-migration nexus empirically, and had to deal with various limitations. Future research therefore needs to decide whether its main findings – the push factor explanation is empirically valid while the pull factor explanation is not – are robust, and how far they apply beyond the Dutch case.

5 Immigration and unemployment

Immigration is one of the constitutive processes of globalization today (Sassen, 2006d: 315; cf. Sassen, 1998: xxi).

We argue that immigration is a powerful example of 'globalization from below' and needs to be integrated into our understanding of global city dynamics. By linking global cities and immigration, this research highlights those cities that are experiencing dramatic socio-cultural changes brought about by large and often diverse streams of immigrants (Benton-Short, Price & Friedman, 2005: 945).

5.1 Introduction

According to the theoretical reasoning concerning the push and pull factors for the new immigration in the global city theoretical framework addressed in the previous chapter, this immigration is driven by economic globalization. This logic was partly corroborated in Chapter 4, as Dutch foreign direct investments were indeed strongly related to immigration flows to cities in the Netherlands from newly-industrializing countries. Given that the central aim in the global city debate is to assess the impact of economic globalization on the social and economic realities of cities, it seems to be overly one-sided to merely examine what drives immigration. This is because immigration is not only a consequence of economic globalization, but also one of its constituting elements (cf. Sassen, 2006d: 315, Sassen, 1998: xxi). As a result, it is often referred to using the abstract term 'the globalization of labour'. Several immigration researchers active in the global city debate consequently recommend treating it as such (Benton-Short et al., 2005), and some even suggest using it as another indicator of the globalness of cities along with the clustering of advanced producer services (Malecki & Ewers, 2007).

Many studies that treat immigration as the globalization of labour assess the tenability of the substitution thesis, which asserts that immigrants can be substitutes for natives and former waves of immigrants with whom they compete on the labour market. By applying classic economic logic to the labour market, the substitution thesis claims that immigration leads to downward pressure on the wages of natives and former waves of immigrants, especially in regulated labour markets, eventually causing the unemployment of these groups. After elaborating on the theoretical logic of the substitution thesis and the findings of empirical tests of this theory in Section 5.2, this chapter will assess the impact of immigration on unemployment among the less educated in Dutch urban labour markets in Section 5.3. The concluding section will discuss the findings of this chapter and answer the sixth research question: *What is the impact of immigration on unemployment among less-educated urbanites?*

5.2 The substitution thesis

5.2.1 The substitution thesis: theory and evidence

The substitution thesis applies a classic economic model of supply and demand to the labour market, with the expectation that immigration, i.e. an increasing labour supply, will reduce the cost of labour (Chiswick, 1982; Johnson, 1980). Consequently, immigration will lead to a fall in the wages of the workers with whom the immigrants are competing, or, in the case of inflexible labour markets, to an increased likelihood of unemployment.

Most studies in this field of research focus on the United States, but a substantial number also address Western European countries. In 2005, Longhi et al. produced an inventory of the few dozens of studies on the impact of immigration on wages up to 2003, and then analysed their findings in a meta-study. A few years later, Okkerse (2008) followed with a review of the findings of studies on the substitution thesis up to 2005, stating that the 'approaches and results [of her study] complement the ones discussed in the meta-analysis carried out by Longhi et al. (2005) on wage effects of migration' (2008: 2). This is because Okkerse's study was more comprehensive, since it took 'a broader definition of labour market effects' (ibid.), as it 'also question[ed] the effects of immigration on labour participation and on the likelihood of being employed or unemployed' (ibid.). As such, her review included almost all the empirical studies on the substitution thesis published up to 2005.

Despite their different approaches and scope the two studies come to the same conclusions. Firstly, 'immigration negatively affects wages of less-skilled labourers and earlier immigrants' (Okkerse, 2008: 24), especially the latter, as 'immigrants are more in competition with other immigrants than with natives' (Longhi et al., 2005: 472). It does, however, need to be stressed that these effects are very small, as emphasized by the authors themselves (Longhi et al., 2005). Secondly, 'the probability that immigrants increase unemployment is low in the short run and zero in the long run' (Okkerse, 2008: 24). In short, it can be concluded that the substitution thesis holds true in general: immigration depresses the wages of lower-skilled natives and immigrants – especially the latter. The overall impact is, nevertheless, weak and the employment effects wither over time.

The research on the substitution thesis that appeared after 2005, or was not included in the meta-studies addressed above, essentially produced the same results: no impact (Arrasco, Jimeno & Ortega, 2008; Boubtane, Coulibaly & Rault, 2013; Catanzarite, 2003; Cohen-Goldner & Paserman, 2006; Islam, 2008), or a weak, negative impact on the wages or likelihood of employment of the low-skilled (Borjas, 2006; Bratsberg & Raaum, 2012; Damette & Fromentin, 2013; Islam, 2009; Ferderman, Harrington & Krynski, 2006; Wilson & Jaynes, 2000; for a more substantial effect, see: Glitz, 2012; Steinhardt, 2011). This impact is, however, somewhat stronger on the jobs and wages of (former waves of) immigrants or ethnic minorities, as these groups are the most direct competitors to immigrants on the labour market (Catanzarite & Aguilera, 2002; Reed & Danziger, 2007; Boustan, 2007).

Consequently, although there is great variety in the findings on the substitution thesis published between 1980 and 2013, the 'overall' results of studies on the issue can be summarized as follows: immigration has a negative impact on both the wages of natives and the immigrants they compete with, especially on the salaries of the latter. Furthermore, this can lead to unemployment for both of these categories, especially in countries with more labour market regulation (Jean & Jimenez, 2007).

On the basis of the theoretical rationale of the substitution thesis, then, the expectation is that the settlement of immigrants in Dutch cities would depress wages and increase the likelihood of unemployment of low-skilled natives and, especially, immigrants. However, there are several indications in the literature which suggest that the extent of this substitution differs from city to city. It is proposed that some types of urban economy absorb supply shocks in labour much better than others, and that, consequently, immigration hardly, or not at all, leads to substitution in the labour market. This might be the reason why: 1) studies on the substitution thesis within the same country produce scattered results, and 2) the overall findings are often weaker than assumed on the basis of the theoretical rationale of the theory.

5.2.2 The substitution thesis and the urban economy

Several of the authors who have assessed the substitution thesis suspect that urban economies differ in the extent to which immigration has an impact on wages or unemployment rates. Card (1990), for instance, examined the thesis using the 'natural experiment' that has become known as the 'Mariel boatlift'. The cause of this event was the 1980 granting of temporary permission for Cubans to leave Cuba. Consequently, within a time span of approximately six months, the Miami labour market experienced at least a seven per cent rise in overall labour supply (this figure was much higher at the bottom of the labour market, as most of the immigrants were unskilled). Despite this major influx of unskilled Cubans, there was very little impact on the wages and unemployment rates of low-skilled natives and former waves of immigrants. Card wondered why this was, as these findings seemingly flew in the face of the classic supply-and-demand logic of the substitution thesis. His suggested answer was that the local economic structure was responsible for mitigating the wage and unemployment effects of increases in labour supply. More specifically, he expected that the strong presence of 'immigrant intensive industries [such as] private household services, hotels and motels, eating and drinking establishments, and business services' in the Miami metropolitan economy was responsible for this outcome (1990: 256; cf. Card, 2005).

Others have made similar arguments. Wilson and Jaynes, for instance, stress that 'the adjustment of local labour markets to immigration may be very quick, particularly if the inflow is modest and the economy is sufficiently diversified to allow for the absorption of immigrants in a variety of sectors' (2000: 159; cf. Catanzarite, 2003; Friedberg & Hunt, 1995). A comparison between Amsterdam and Rotterdam corroborated this logic. In Amsterdam, which has a more service-centred economy than Rotterdam, immigration did not lead to downward pressure on the wages of lower-educated natives and immigrants, but it did in Rotterdam (Van der Waal, 2009, 2013c).

In short, a number of authors of studies on the substitution thesis argue, and several research findings indicate, that cities with a well-developed service sector yield a higher labour demand for less-educated workers than urban economies with a less-developed service economy. Consequently, the former cities are better equipped than the latter to integrate newcomers on the labour market without any consequences for the wages or unemployment risks of natives and earlier waves of immigrants. If this is correct, the classic supply-and-demand logic of the substitution thesis is still essentially accurate, but cannot properly be assessed by only taking the supply side, i.e. immigration, into account. There thus needs to be consideration of the possibility that urban economies might differ in terms of the labour demand for less-educated workers.

These suggestions are completely in line with the findings in Chapter 3 that Dutch cities with the highest employment share in the advanced producer services have the smallest, if any, mismatch between labour demand and supply at the bottom of the labour market. This was interpreted on the basis of the polarization thesis, which claims that this pattern is driven by a high labour demand for low-skilled service workers who occupy the same kind of service jobs that according to Card (1990) in the quote above will absorb shocks in labour supply and, consequently, attenuate substitution in the labour market. The combination of the findings in Chapter 3 and the suggestions of Card and other scholars on the substitution thesis, thus leads to the expectation that immigration has little impact on wages and unemployment in cities with a high share of advanced producer services, as the presence of these services yields a high labour demand for low-skilled workers.

That studies on the tenability of the substitution thesis do not thus far account for the fact that cities differ widely in terms of the demand for low-skilled labour, and that this is driven by differences in the employment share of the advanced producer services, might be the reason why: 1) they discovered scattered results within the same country, and 2) the substitution found at the country level is often rather weak. In the second case, this weak substitution would simply be the average result of (potentially) high substitution in former industrial strongholds and weak or even absent substitution in cities with a high share of employment in the advanced producer services.

The following section will assess whether immigration does indeed lead to less substitution in labour markets with a high share of employment in the advanced producer services. To do this, the impact of immigration on unemployment of less-educated urbanites will be compared among the 22 Dutch metropolitan areas, so as to rigorously test the suggestion that substitution in the labour market due to immigration is lowest in cities with the highest share of employment in the advanced producer services. Here, the first expectation is that immigration leads to unemployment among less-educated urbanites in Dutch cities. If this is correct, *the unemployment rate of less-educated urbanites is highest in Dutch cities with the highest share of immigrants in the population* (Hypothesis 1). Secondly, it is expected that immigration leads to less unemployment in Dutch cities with a high share of advanced producer services than in those with a low share of these services. If this is accurate, *the positive relationship between immigrant shares and the unemployment rate of less-educated urbanites is smaller in Dutch cities with a high employment share in the advanced producer services than in Dutch cities with a low employment share in the advanced producer services* (Hypothesis 2).

5.3 Assessing the substitution thesis on unemployment

In order to examine whether labour market substitution due to immigration occurs in Dutch cities, and whether that substitution is less significant in the most service-oriented locations, there is again a need for multilevel modelling, just as in Chapter 3. To do this, the dataset used in that chapter will be utilized again, although the time period now is two years shorter. This is because the *unemployment rate among the less educated* is measured two years later than the independent variables. This is a common research practice in studies on the impact of immigration on wages (see Longhi et al., 2005), as the unemployment effects of immigration will not reveal themselves immediately. Accordingly, the first model in Table 5.1 replicates the final model in Table 3.4 in order to control for the issue of whether the shorter time span does indeed not alter the central findings of Chapter 3, i.e. the unemployment rate among the less educated is lowest in cities with the highest employment shares in the advanced producer services, as predicted on the basis of the polarization thesis. Model 1 demonstrates that this is indeed the case. The only difference with the findings in Chapter 3

Table 5.1 Unemployment rate of the less educated in the 22 Dutch metropolitan areas (1998-2007), explained by the employment shares in the advanced producer services, the hotel and catering industry, the cultural industries, and immigrant shares (multilevel regression analysis; entries are regression coefficients; estimation: maximum likelihood)

	Model 1	Model 2	Model 3
Independents	*B*	*B*	*B*
Constant	5.47**	4.69**	-2.36
Advanced producer services	-0.13*	-0.15**	0.14
Cultural industries	0.54*	0.42	0.49*
Hotel and catering industry	0.41	0.13	0.21
Immigrant share		0.12***	0.44**
Advanced producer services * immigrant share			-0.01*
Controls			
Age 15-24	-0.15*	-0.11*	-0.10
Variance metropolitan level (*N* = 22)	1.21	1.23	1.17
Variance year level (*N* = 10)	1.36	1.31	1.30
Log likelihood	-404.24	-396.98	-393.78

Source: StatLine CBS (own calculations)
*$p < 0.05$; **$p < 0.01$; ***$p < 0.001$

is that the cultural industries have a positive, significant effect – instead of no impact at all – on this unemployment rate, albeit that it is only just significant.

In Model 2, I entered *immigrant share*, which, in accordance with Hypothesis 1 deduced from the substitution thesis, yields a positive and significant coefficient: in metropolitan areas with a high share of immigrants, the unemployment rate of less-educated urbanites is higher. Nevertheless, the question remains as to whether the impact of immigration on the unemployment rate of less-educated urbanites is weaker, or even absent, in the most service-oriented urban economies. To provide an answer, the interaction effect of *immigrant share* with *advanced producer services* was entered into Model 3. The coefficient was negative and significant, which means that the impact of immigration on unemployment is less in cities with a high employment share in the advanced producer services than in those with a low employment share in those services. This corroborates the central expectation of this chapter, i.e. Hypothesis 2.

Figure 5.1 is a graphic representation of the interaction effect between *immigrant share* and *advanced producer services*. Its horizontal axis depicts the employment share in these services, while the vertical axis indicates the unemployment rate of less-educated urbanites. The lines represent the unemployment rates predicted on the basis of Model 3 in Table 5.1, under two conditions: if the immigrant share is 1) 8% (dotted line), and 2) 37% (solid line). It should be noted that these two conditions have not been randomly chosen, but represent the lowest and highest scores of the variable *immigrant share* in the dataset. The grey areas indicate the confidence intervals. To start with the first condition (the dotted line), in the case of an 8% immigrant share in the working population, all the urban economies under study are able to absorb these workers. Yet, with the highest immigrant share in the dataset as an example, they clearly cannot. For cities with the highest employment shares in the advanced producer services, these high immigrant shares can still be absorbed on the labour market, but this is clearly not the case for those with low employment shares in those services. In the latter cities, which are represented by the left-hand side of Figure 5.1, high immigrant shares lead to labour market substitution, as the high unemployment rate among the less educated on that side demonstrates.

Figure 5.1 Unemployment rate of less-educated urbanites as predicted by the employment shares in the advanced producer services in the 22 Dutch metropolitan areas, if the immigrant share is 8% (dotted line) and 37% (solid line)

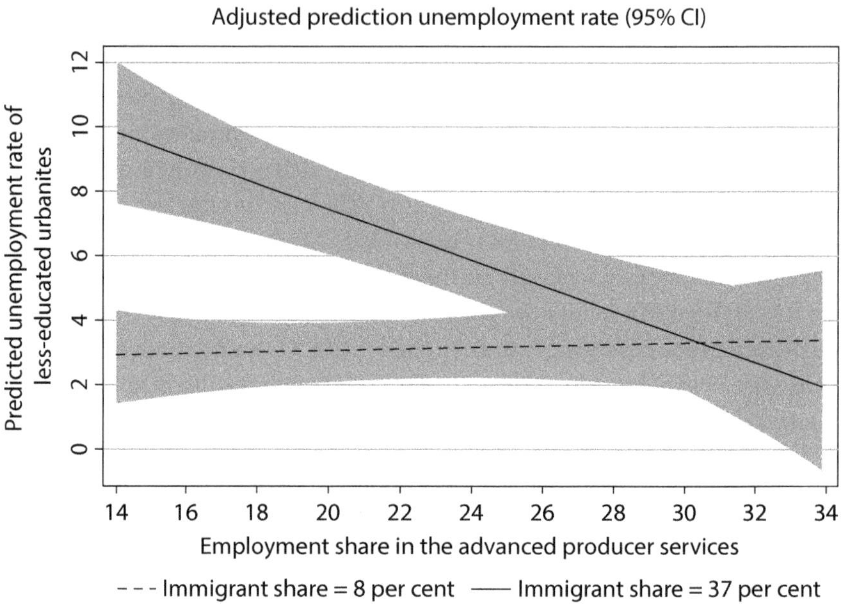

5.4 Conclusions

This chapter started with the observation that the examination of immigration in the global city theoretical framework, and therefore the global city debate, has a one-sided focus: it only considers what drives immigration from newly-industrializing countries to cities in the advanced economies, and argues that this immigration is driven by pull and push factors that stem from the new international division of labour. This one-sided focus seems remarkable given that the global city theoretical framework, which spurred the global city debate, was formulated to explain the impact of the current phase of economic globalization on the social and economic realities of cities. This is because immigration cannot only be considered to be a consequence, but also one of globalization's constitutive elements: the globalization of labour.

It is claimed that this globalization of labour has an impact on urban labour markets, and the theoretical rationale of this effect is laid down in substitution theory. This thesis applies classic economic supply-and-demand logic to the labour market, and claims that immigration leads to supply shocks in labour that lower the price for workers and, ultimately, leads to the unemployment of those with whom immigrants are competing. As a consequence, this chapter assessed the empirical validity of this claim so as to answer the sixth research question: *What is the impact of immigration on urban labour markets?* This was achieved by assessing the impact of immigration on the unemployment rate of competitors on the labour market, i.e. less-educated urbanites, be they natives or (former waves of) immigrants.

Several of the scholars working with the substitution thesis suspect that this impact is weaker in service-oriented urban economies, due to a higher demand for labour. This expectation is fully in line with the findings in chapters 3 and 4. Chapter 3 demonstrated that the labour demand for low-skilled service workers is high in cities with a high share of employment in the advanced producer services, and that, consequently, the unemployment rate of less-educated urbanites in those cities is low. As a result, the expectation is that if the substitution thesis holds true, substitution between immigrants on the one hand and less-educated natives and former waves of immigrants on the other will be least significant in cities with a high share of employment in the advanced producer services, and most significant in cities with a low share of this type of employment.

This chapter assessed this expectation, which proved to be essentially correct: immigration only leads to a game of musical chairs at the bottom of the labour market in the less service-oriented urban economies, i.e. in urban economies with low employment shares in the advanced producer services. This is because the demand for labour in these cities is simply not high enough to absorb the less-educated labour supply settled there. Consequently, immigration aggravates the already scarce labour-market opportunities in these urban economies for immigrants and less-educated natives alike. In strong service-centred urban economies, on the other hand, the labour demand is high enough to absorb labour supply shocks due to immigration.

Like the discovery that the unemployment effect of immigration is stronger in more regulated economies (Jean & Jimenez, 2007), the finding here is in line with the classic supply-and-demand logic of the substitution thesis. This is because labour demand, just like labour supply, varies across cities. Furthermore, by also modelling the demand side, i.e. the type of urban economy, this study was able to interpret varying levels of substitution across cities according to the substitution thesis. This proves that instead of merely discussing methods and statistics (cf. Card, 2005: 321), it is fruitful to thoroughly consider the theoretical underpinnings of the substitution thesis when looking for a cause of the scattered results that research on its tenability reports. It should be noted, however, that this is not to say that the use of proper methods and statistics is unimportant (cf. Longhi et al., 2005: 471); instead, the point is that scattered results can be in line with theoretical expectations rather than being statistical or empirical aberrations. As the nature and strength of the demand for labour differs between countries and between cities, the impact of immigration – i.e. shocks in labour supply – on unemployment differs accordingly between countries and between cities. That for some local labour markets, namely those with low labour demand, there is an impact of immigration on unemployment, while for others, i.e. those with high labour demand, there is not, is thus in line, instead of at odds, with the substitution thesis. By somehow modelling both local labour demand and local labour supply – instead of assuming that local demand is the same across cities – this can be accounted for when studying the empirical tenability of substitution theory.

As well as providing a potential explanation for the scattered results of previous studies on the substitution thesis, the research findings in this study can explain why country-level research on this theory often identifies weak substitution effects. This is because these weak effects might be the net result of underestimations of substitution in cities with low employment shares in the advanced producer services, and overestimations in places with high employment shares in those services. Such weak effects often leave the authors of these studies wondering how this is possible, as the substitution logic seems to be so self-evident. Again, just like scattered results, weak effects might be the result of a research format that is not in accordance with the logic of the substitution thesis, as it does not model local differences in labour demand, but merely local differences in immigrant labour supply.

Consider, for instance, the only study on the impact of immigration on wages for the Netherlands as a whole, which was unable to model local differences in labour demand due to data deficiencies. Accordingly, in that study, 'the participation rate is assumed to be identically distributed across local labour markets for each ethnic minority group' (Zorlu & Hartog, 2005: 120). The research concluded that 'the effect of immigrants on natives' wages is genuinely small' (2005: 134), as 'a 10 percent increase of ethnic minorities from non-EU countries decreases the earnings of low-skilled workers by 0.42%' (2005: 120-1, cf. the meta-study by Longhi et al., 2005: 472). Such conclusions are, in the first place, misleading, as they imply that the extent of substitution between immigrants and natives or former waves of immigrants can be effectively measured by simply modelling the immigrant share. They are also problematic because they depict substitution to be modest, while their findings are in fact probably deflated, because there are no substitution effects in cities with high employment shares in the advanced producer services (cf. Van der Waal, 2009, 2013c).

All this being said, the findings of this chapter lead to another question: Why do immigrants settle in cities where the labour demand is low? This flies in the face of the market logic that is often assumed to be driving migration to the advanced economies. In accordance with this market logic, although Dutch cities with high employment shares in the advanced producer services do indeed have higher immigrant shares in their population (Pearson's $r = 0.291, p < 0.0005, N = 220$), the settlement of immigrants is not completely determined by labour demand, or their unemployment rates would not differ between cities. Non-market logic such as the influence of a decommodified housing market, but also kinship and ethnic or social ties with former waves of immigrants, are probably responsible for this pattern (cf. Zorlu & Mulder, 2008).

Overall, it seems safe to conclude that future studies on the substitution thesis need to take into account the fact that urban economies differ in terms of labour demand, and that the settlement of immigrants does not necessarily follow labour market logic. If these studies do this, the research format will be more in accordance with the theoretical underpinnings of the substitution thesis, and are therefore likely to yield findings that are easier to interpret. Such a format might even become more salient, as cities, at least in the Netherlands, diverge in the extent to which advanced producer services cluster, as we saw in Chapter 2. As this clustering proves to be the driving force for the demand for labour for less-educated urbanites, local differences in the extent to which immigration leads to labour market substitution are therefore likely to grow in importance.

6 Conclusions and discussion

The globalization of economic activity entails a new type of organizational structure. To capture this theoretically and empirically requires, correspondingly, a new type of conceptual architecture (Sassen, 2001: xviii).

6.1 Introduction

This chapter discusses the findings in the previous chapters and their theoretical and empirical implications as elicited by the six research questions that guided this study (Section 6.2). This is followed by a discussion of to what extent the theoretical notions in the global city theoretical framework and debate help us to understand the impact of the current phase of economic globalization on the social and economic realities of cities (Section 6.3). The concluding section discusses the alleged political implications of this study.

6.2 After the unravelling: theoretical and empirical implications

Sassen formulated the global city theoretical framework, namely the new conceptual architecture referred to in the quote at the beginning of this chapter, because previous explanations of changes in urban labour markets were considered to be inadequate when it came to understanding the impact of the recent phase of economic globalization on the social and economic realities of cities (Sassen, 1994, 2000, 2001, 2006a, 2012). The framework 1) argues that the new type of organizational structure that characterizes the current phase of globalization, i.e. the new international division of labour that stems from the practice of outsourcing parts of the production process from the advanced economies to newly-industrializing countries, has brought major changes to urban labour markets in the advanced economies, and 2) provides a theoretical rationale to explain how this came about.

Even though this rationale is comprised of several theoretical notions that were formulated in the 1980s and early 1990s, it is not yet clear whether, as its author claimed, it helps us to understand the impact of the current phase of economic globalization on the social and economic realities of cities. In the introductory chapter, it was argued that what is largely responsible for this theoretical stagnation is the fact that the global city theoretical framework is not a testable middle-range theory, but rather a grand composition, i.e. an agglomeration of integrated theories, propositions, and expectations. The bulk of empirical studies in the global city debate that it spurred thus merely used it as a frame of reference to interpret urban developments that were thought to be the consequence of economic globalization. As a result, much has been said, but little is known, about the impact of economic globalization on urban labour markets in the global city debate.

This study therefore aimed to discover whether the central theoretical notions in the global city theoretical framework, and their alternative interpretations in the global city debate, do indeed help us to understand the impact of the current phase of economic globalization on the social and economic realities of cities. To do this, it was necessary to provide answers to six questions. As a consequence, the theoretical notions of the global city debate needed to be examined in order to uncover whether they are adequate when it comes to assessing the impact of globalization. This examination often called for those notions to be addressed in relation to competing ideas. The sections that follow will discuss the theoretical and empirical implications of the findings of this endeavour, and what they mean for urban labour markets in the advanced economies.

6.2.1 The changing economic base of cities

Chapter 2 first addressed the question: *Does the economic base of cities in general increasingly resemble the economic base of global cities?* This was necessary because it is often assumed in the global city debate that global cities wear the future guise of other cities. Strikingly, this is in contrast to what is asserted in the global city theoretical framework, which claims that the clustering of advanced producer services in the most service-oriented cities – whether they are global cities or regional nodes – feeds on the deindustrialization of former industrial strongholds. The suggested reason for this is that the management and coordination of the manufacturing that was previously conducted in those strongholds now takes place in global cities or regional nodes. As a result, it is anticipated that the employment share in the advanced producer services will increase significantly more in global cities and regional nodes than in their industrial counterparts. In other words, according to the global city theoretical framework, the economic base of many cities, most notably former industrial strongholds, *decreasingly* resembles the economic base of global and other service-oriented cities that function as regional nodes. Chapter 2 demonstrated that this is precisely what happened in the Netherlands between 1995 and 2008. The first research question addressed in this study therefore needs to be answered in the negative.

Previous studies on the changing economic base of cities in the United States and the former Federal Republic of Germany in the 1980s had pointed in the same direction (Kasarda 1985; Kasarda & Friedrichs, 1985, 1986). Indeed, in those countries, the transition to a post-industrial economy seemed to affect cities unequally in the same way as in the current research: the former industrial strongholds lagged behind when it came to employment growth in the advanced producer services. This suggests that there is a general phenomenon in advanced economies. Nevertheless, which former industrial strongholds will lag behind the most, and which service-oriented cities will see their share of employment in the advanced producer services increase the most, is of course still an empirical question for any given country. Moreover, the mechanism that allegedly accounts for the diverging fortunes of former industrial strongholds vis-à-vis service-oriented cities, i.e. 'predatory growth' where the advanced producer services in the latter thrive at the cost of the former's deindustrialization, calls for further empirical scrutiny.

The second research question addressed in Chapter 2 asked: *Does international outsourcing drive deindustrialization and the clustering of advanced producer services in cities?* In the global city theoretical framework and debate, it is assumed that deindustrialization and the clustering of advanced producer services in cities in the advanced economies is caused by international outsourcing. According to this argument, those cities experienced substantial falls in their employment share in manufacturing because large elements of industrial production have been outsourced to newly-industrializing countries. The management of the globally dispersed production chains of multinationals that result from this practice is claimed to be too complex to be handled by these multinationals' headquarters themselves. As a result, this work is contracted out to advanced producer services such as law, accountancy, and consultancy firms, which therefore cluster in cities. Although this argument was initially formulated for a limited number of global cities, in the global city debate it is considered to be relevant for all cities in the advanced economies. In short, deindustrialization and the clustering of advanced producer services in cities in general are attributed to international outsourcing and, subsequently, economic globalization.

This proved to be a crude overstatement, as it combines arguments on deindustrialization that are empirically unsubstantiated with those on the clustering of advanced producer services that cannot be applied to cities in the advanced economies in general. In terms of deindustrialization, the bulk of the studies on its causes indicate that it is not really driven by international outsourcing. Instead, the combination of technological change and the change in demand from goods to services is responsible for the declining share of employment in industry in cities in the advanced economies. These findings falsify the argument in the global city theoretical framework concerning the link between economic globalization and deindustrialization. As the bulk of the studies in the global city debate that map deindustrialization do not assess its causes, but simply interpret them on the basis of arguments in the global city theoretical framework, the invalid argument that deindustrialization largely occurred due to the outsourcing of production to low-wage countries is reproduced over and over again. It must be noted, however, that this finding does not imply that deindustrialization has no link to economic globalization whatsoever, as technological change could of course be driven by international competition. Nevertheless, it does demonstrate that the dominant claim in the global city debate, i.e. that deindustrialization came about due to international outsourcing, is empirically unsubstantiated.

When it comes to the clustering of advanced producer services, this is only driven by international outsourcing in so far as it concerns the services that cluster in global cities to meet the demand for the skills required by multinationals' headquarters to manage their globally dispersed production process. That part of the advanced producer services in global cities is involved in this production is beyond doubt, as can easily be observed in places like Manhattan (New York), Canary Wharf (London), and the *Zuidas* (Amsterdam). Yet, this does not mean that all professionals in the advanced producer services in global cities are involved in producing the global control capacities for the headquarters of multinationals. In addition, as shown in Chapter 2, many former industrial strongholds and cities that function as regional nodes have also experienced growing employment shares in the advanced producer services in recent decades. That the clustering of these services not only manifests itself in global cities, but also in places that function as regional nodes in an attenuated form, as argued in the global city theoretical framework (Sassen, 2000: 139, 2006a: 193, 2006c: x), has thus been corroborated in this study. Nonetheless, this clustering is not driven by international outsourcing, and the link with economic globalization therefore seems to be missing. If, however, there is such a link, it is at least not in accordance with the argument by which it is interpreted in the global city debate.

In short, Research Question 2 – *Does international outsourcing drive deindustrialization and the clustering of advanced producer services in cities?* – must be answered in the negative. This is because international outsourcing barely drives deindustrialization at all and only part of the clustering of advanced producer services in global cities. Why, then, does employment in the advanced producer services also increase in former industrial strongholds and regional nodes? This was not assessed in this study. However, I think that what is crucial here is that the vertical disintegration of firms that led to 'the new organisational structure' that characterizes the current phase of economic globalization (Sassen, 2001: xviii), i.e. the new international division of labour, has more causes than lower wage levels in less-developed economies, namely a quest for efficiency that does not necessarily entail economic globalization.

Many consider a vertically disintegrated firm to be more efficient for producing goods and services; by sticking to their core business, much of what was previously produced in-house in vertically integrated firms is now provided by other companies, most notably those providing advanced producer services. The question of whether this contracting out is indeed more efficient, and how this greater efficiency precisely comes about, is beyond the scope of this study and is also not crucial here. What is important, however, is that contracting out leads to a new organizational structure, which is not driven by international outsourcing and manifests itself on a geographical scale other than the new organizational structure to which the global city theoretical framework refers.

The question that remains concerns the extent to which this argument applies beyond the Dutch case. I see no reason why this should be different for advanced economies other than the Netherlands. This is because, ultimately, it all boils down to the finding that merely the share of employment in the advanced producer services in global cities that is involved in the production of the capabilities to manage globally dispersed production processes can be directly linked to international outsourcing. However, most of the cities in advanced economies are, just like in the Netherlands, former industrial strongholds and regional nodes where the clustering of advanced producer services has no link with international outsourcing, but is more likely to be driven by regional or national processes.

6.2.2 Advanced producer services and labour demand

The argument in the global city theoretical framework that the clustering of advanced producer services has been the primary driving force of urban employment in recent decades is undisputed. That these services employ a disproportionate share of highly educated professionals compared to other sectors, most notably those that were dominant in the industrial/Fordist era, is also undeniable. What is, however, contested is whether the clustering of advanced producer services leads to a polarized occupational hierarchy, as predicted by Sassen's polarization thesis, or to a professionalized occupational hierarchy, as expected by Hamnett's professionalization theory. The crucial difference between these theses is that, according to the former, the clustering of advanced producer services leads to a high labour demand for low-skilled service workers, while according to the latter its consequence is a low labour demand for these employees. On the basis of the polarization thesis, it would thus be anticipated that the lowest unemployment rate among less-educated urbanites would be found in cities with the highest employment share in these services, while on the basis of the professionalization thesis the expectation would be that it is the other way around.

In various ways, dozens of studies have assessed whether the polarization or professionalization of urban labour markets occurred from the first formulations of the polarization and professionalization theses onwards (see Table A1 in Appendix A). The two options were identified on several occasions, seemingly without a clear pattern as to why some studies found a polarized labour market structure while others identified a professionalized version. A previous study on Dutch cities concerned a comparison of Amsterdam with Rotterdam and found a polarized and a professionalized occupational hierarchy, respectively (Burgers & Musterd, 2002). As the share of professionals in Amsterdam is substantially higher than in Rotterdam, the authors suspected that this finding could be explained by the theoretical reasoning behind the polarization thesis (ibid.).

This thesis asserts that the presence of the advanced producer services yields a high labour demand for low-skilled service workers by a direct and an indirect mechanism. The first pertains to the low-skilled service workers supporting the production process, such as cleaners, clerks, and security staff. The indirect effect, however, concerns the demand for workers like caterers, dog-walkers, and nannies, due to the 24/7 work schedules of the professionals employed in the advanced producer services. If this is correct, it is only in cities with a very high share of employment in these services, and consequently a very high share of professionals employed in them, that the occupational hierarchy will be polarized. As a result, in cities with a low share of advanced producer services, the share of the professionals is not large enough to yield a high demand for low-skilled service workers, and the occupational hierarchy will thus be professionalized instead of polarized.

Yet, although this sounds very plausible, Burgers and Musterd's study could not provide a litmus test for the empirical tenability of the polarization thesis, as it only assessed two cities. Like the bulk of studies in the global city debate, which examine the occupational hierarchy in one or two cities, it could therefore not determine whether the clustering of advanced producer services is indeed the driving force for this high labour demand for less-educated urbanites. As a consequence, this needed to be tested by a comparative framework, and Chapter 3 did just that by asking the question: *What is the impact of the clustering of advanced producer services on the unemployment rate of less-educated urbanites?* The chapter found that, in accordance with the polarization thesis, the lowest unemployment rates among less-educated urbanites exist in Dutch cities with the highest shares of employment in the advanced producer services. This is not a Dutch idiosyncrasy, as previous studies on cities in the former Federal Republic of Germany and the United States (Kasarda, 1985; Kasarda & Friedrichs, 1985, 1986) produced similar results. These studies demonstrated that cities with a low share of employment in the advanced producer services generate the fewest labour market opportunities for the less educated. It must be noted, however, that only the direct effect outlined above was empirically substantiated.

After finding that the impact of the clustering of advanced producer services on the unemployment of less-educated urbanites needs to be understood according to the polarization thesis, and not professionalization, theory, Chapter 3 focused on the issue of whether that productivist interpretation still applies if confronted with a consumerist alternative. The latter was developed on the basis of the ideas of, most notably, Richard Florida and Terry Nichols Clark, and claimed that the settlement of advanced producer services is partly driven by the lifestyles and cultural preferences of the professionals they employ. The idea is that these professionals prefer to settle in cities that are rich in cultural amenities, with their employers simply following them in the quest to find the most productive labour force. The consumerist alternative to the polarization thesis also claims that the clustering of cultural industries yields a high labour demand for low-skilled service workers, in a similar way to polarization theory: directly to support the production process and indirectly to cater to the lifestyles of the professionals employed in cultural industries. Yet, Chapter 3 demonstrated that these industries do not affect the unemployment rates of less-educated urbanites and are barely responsible for the settlement of advanced producer services. Accordingly, notwithstanding the increasing salience of consumerist theorizing in urban studies at large, the labour market structure and unemployment rates that accompany it still need to be understood according to the productivist polarization thesis, at least in the Netherlands.

Two questions remain: 1) How does this outcome relate to previous findings on the polarization and/or professionalization thesis in the global city debate? and 2) How far do these conclusions travel beyond the Dutch case? In terms of the first issue, all the previous studies on European global cities that used a similar strategy to Burgers and Musterd (2002) did identify a professionalized occupational hierarchy. However, the studies on Amsterdam (Hamnett, 1994a), London (Hamnett, 1994b, 1996a, 2004), and Paris (Rhein, 1996) used data from the 1980s, while Burgers and Musterd's data concerned the 1990s. In the 1980s, the employment share in the advanced producer services might have been too small to yield enough labour demand for less-educated service workers. The fact that Hamnett found a professionalized occupational hierarchy in Amsterdam in the 1980s, while Burgers and Musterd found a polarized version there in the 1990s also points in this direction. The expectation would thus be that the occupational hierarchies of London, Paris, and other European global cities have become polarized by now, although this has not yet been documented. As far as I know, other than Burgers and Musterd's study, there is no research on occupational change in European global cities that applies the same method with post-1990 data. That recent studies on London (May et al., 2007) and Athens (Maloutas, 2007) using a slightly different method, but recent data, have identified a polarized occupational hierarchy does, however, strongly suggest that the occupational hierarchy of European global cities will be polarized by now.

In short, all the available evidence suggests that 1) the occupational hierarchy in European global cities has become polarized by now, and 2) it is indeed the clustering of advanced producer services that drives the high labour demand for less-educated urbanites, as asserted in the polarization thesis. Yet, this does not mean that the occupational hierarchy in cities in the advanced economies in general will be polarized by now. Given Chapter 2's finding that the employment share in the advanced producer services in former industrial strongholds increases at a much slower pace than in the most service-oriented cities, it is very likely that the former still have a professionalized occupational hierarchy, while that of the latter is polarized. The employment share in the advanced producer services in former industrial strongholds is simply not high enough to yield a high labour demand for less-educated service workers. Consequently, those cities still have high unemployment rates.

Again, just as argued in the previous section, the widely-held assumption in the global city debate that global cities like New York and Amsterdam wear the future guise of cities lower down the urban hierarchy (e.g. Burgers, 1996; Friedmann & Wolff, 1982; Mollenkopf, 2009; Mollenkopf & Castells, 1992; Vaattovaara & Kortteinen, 2003) is highly problematic. This hypothesis is questionable not only because the economic base of most cities becomes less instead of more similar to that of global cities, but also because all the available evidence suggests that the occupational hierarchy of cities *in general* will be neither polarized nor professionalized. Instead, the polarization thesis will apply to cities with the highest share of employment in the advanced producer services (most notably, global cities), while the professionalization version will pertain to cities with the lowest share of employment in those services (most notably, former industrial strongholds).

The author of the professionalization thesis, Chris Hamnett, has already suggested that the occupational hierarchy of some cities will be polarized due to the clustering of advanced producer services, while it will be professionalized in other cities. However, he came to this conclusion on the basis of a point other than the one confirmed in this study. In particular, he argued that the polarization thesis is 'American-centric' (Hamnett, 1994a, 1994b, 1996a, 1996b, 1998, 2004; cf. White, 1998), as global cities in the United States combine a high immigrant influx with a highly deregulated labour market, which their counterparts outside the US do not. Consequently, it is only in the former that the high labour demand for cheap service workers can be met by an abundant supply of low-skilled labour. As a result, Hamnett expected the occupational hierarchy in global cities in the United States to be polarized, while it would be professionalized in more regulated European labour markets. In short, according to Hamnett, the extent to which urban labour markets are regulated will determine whether the occupational hierarchy in global cities will be polarized or professionalized.

On the basis of the findings in this study, I also suggest that both polarization and professionalization will occur, but not according to Hamnett's scenario; my conclusion is that in both deregulated and regulated advanced economies, cities with the highest share of employment in the advanced producer services (most notably, global cities) will have a polarized occupational hierarchy, while those with the lowest share of employment in these services (most notably, former industrial strongholds) will have a professionalized version. The question of whether the share of employment in the advanced producer services will keep on increasing in the latter type of city, and will consequently lead to a polarized occupational hierarchy, is an empirical one. The findings in Chapter 2 that this increase occurs in the former industrial strongholds at a much slower pace than in the least industrial cities suggests that this will certainly take some time, meaning that the high unemployment rates that these cities have to face will persist in the near future.

6.2.3 The new international division of labour and immigration

The global city theoretical framework claims that the current phase of economic globalization spurs *new* migration flows from less-developed countries to cities in the advanced economies. As such, it does not compete with classic migration theories that revolve around underdevelopment and poverty, which essentially claim that this migration is driven by the desire of migrants to improve their economic fortunes. Instead, it is argued that these 'classic' migration flows are now accompanied by new ones driven by foreign direct investment in newly-industrializing countries and the clustering of advanced producer services in cities, most notably global cities in the advanced economies.

These investments in newly-industrializing countries are postulated as causing an uprooting of people, which constitutes the *push factor* for new migration flows. It is claimed that these investments, in the form of production sites that are often referred to as export processing zones, spur labour migration from rural hinterlands to coastal and/or urban regions. Consequently, people who were previously embedded in traditional work structures become wage labourers at these production sites, which produce goods and services for export to the advanced economies. The combination of the capitalist logic of wage labour and the production of goods and services for the advanced economies makes these workers aware of the possibility of migrating to these economies to improve their economic position. As foreign direct investment leads to cultural links between sending and receiving countries, such migration is supposed to precisely mirror the investment flows, i.e. from the countries that receive investment to those from where these investments originate.

According to the global city theoretical framework, the *pull factor* for this new immigration is the high labour demand for low-skilled service workers in cities in the advanced economies, especially in global cities where, according to the polarization thesis, such high labour demand exists.

Even though these new push and pull factors were formulated in the early 1980s, they have not yet been assessed together. In the global city debate, they are simply assumed to be valid. This study, however, filled this lacuna by assessing these factors for migration from newly-industrializing countries to Dutch cities, and did so by considering the question: *Can the new immigration to cities in the advanced economies be explained by foreign direct investments?* It was discovered that, controlled for classic migration patterns that revolve around differences in the state of economic development between countries, the greatest increase in new migration flows stemmed from nations where Dutch foreign direct investments increased the most. Although this is completely in accordance with the push factor argument in the global city theoretical framework, it should be interpreted with care for three reasons.

In the first place, although I tried to control for this problem by excluding the estimated number of knowledge workers, the increase in immigration involved both highly educated and less-educated immigrants. Unfortunately, it was not possible to only select the latter, although these clearly are the immigrants addressed in the push and pull factors in Sassen's FDI-migration nexus. Secondly, the causality of the relationship that was identified is unclear, particularly because another theory asserts that it is reversed, claiming that the information that immigrants have concerning investment opportunities in their homeland is what drives foreign direct investments. If this is correct, immigration is not driven by foreign direct investments, but vice versa. Thirdly, the applied method cannot reveal whether the immigration from newly-industrializing countries to the advanced economies is indeed driven by 'uprooting', as claimed in the global city theoretical framework. Future ethnographic research in export processing zones could uncover whether this mechanism does indeed exist, as this is way beyond the scope of this study.

The findings of the analyses on the pull factor are less difficult to interpret. According to the global city theoretical framework, a high labour demand for low-skilled service workers due to the clustering of advanced producer services is what pulls immigrants from newly-industrializing countries to cities in the advanced economies. Accordingly, the second question addressed in Chapter 4 was: *Does the clustering of advanced producer services attract immigrant labour from newly-industrializing countries?* If it does, the biggest increase in the number of those immigrants will be found in cities with the greatest rise in employment in the advanced producer services. Although a plausible explanation, this reasoning was not empirically valid with respect to the Dutch case. Indeed, the labour demand for the less educated is higher in cities with the highest share of employment in the advanced producer services, but this does not function as a pull factor for new immigrant groups; there was no relationship whatsoever between the increase in new immigrant groups and the rise in this type of employment.

What, then, do these findings on Dutch cities mean for cities in the advanced economies in general? Of course, advanced economies differ in their regulatory framework concerning immigration, which will clearly influence its nature and extent. This does not, however, undermine the theoretical reasoning of the FDI-migration nexus, but merely influences the extent to which it exists. In addition, the empirical validity of the underlying uprooting mechanism of this push factor and the causal direction of the relationship between FDI and migration flows call for closer scrutiny. If, for the sake of the argument, one assumes that this mechanism does indeed exist, and that the causal direction is that FDI spurs migration instead of the other way around, I do not see why this push factor would not also lead to migration to advanced economies other than the Netherlands. In fact, three studies found the same relationship for the United States (Arocay & Maloney, 2005; Ricketts, 1987; Yang, 1998), which also points in this direction.

I expect the findings on the pull factor to travel less well beyond the Netherlands, at least not to countries with less regulated labour and housing markets. After all, the pull factor for new immigration flows in the global city theoretical framework is a latter-day version of classic labour market logic. It is thus very likely that in less regulated labour markets, such as in the United States or the United Kingdom, the settlement of immigrants will be more strongly driven by labour demand than in the Netherlands, where people are less dependent on their labour power for their subsistence. In the Netherlands and many other European countries with regulated labour and housing markets, it is therefore likely that considerations other than labour market opportunities will have a substantial impact on the decisions of immigrants about where to settle.

6.2.4 The impact of immigration on urban labour markets

Sassen formulated the global city theoretical framework because, in the current phase of economic globalization, the old concepts by which 'sociologists have tended to study cities (...) are no longer sufficient' (Sassen, 1994: xiii). Yet, this research revealed that this theoretical framework is only part of the story, and has ironically also obscured, rather than revealed, the impact of certain aspects of economic globalization on urban labour markets. The focus of the global city theoretical framework is on the hallmark of the current phase of economic globalization, namely international outsourcing and the new international division of labour that stems from it. In this framework, immigration is primarily considered to be a result, instead of a central element, of economic globalization. However, immigration is also one of economic globalization's constitutive elements, namely the globalization of labour, and many therefore advocate treating it as such in the global city debate. In the wider globalization literature, it is common practice to assess the impact of immigration on the labour market on the basis of the substitution thesis, which asserts that new influxes of immigrants can lead to declining wages and unemployment among less-educated natives and former waves of immigrants.

As the global city theoretical framework is built on the assumption that immigration from less-developed economies to cities in the advanced economies is driven by a high labour demand for low-skilled service workers, the fact that the substitution thesis is overlooked in the global city debate does not seem to be problematic. Indeed, if this is correct, it is unlikely that immigration would lead to substitution in the labour market. Nevertheless, the economic base of many cities in the advanced economies does not become similar to that of global cities, and so not all of the former yield a high labour demand for low-skilled service workers. This, combined with the fact that, at least in the Netherlands, the settlement of immigrants is not completely driven by labour market considerations, makes it less likely that there will be no substitution between immigrants and natives or former waves of immigrants on the labour market. The blind spot with respect to this substitution in the global city debate is not, therefore, really justified. Accordingly, Chapter 5 considered the question: *What is the impact of immigration on unemployment among less-educated urbanites?*

The analyses in Chapter 5 revealed that immigration does lead to substitution in urban labour markets. As the labour supply increases due to immigration, the labour demand for less-educated urbanites rises at a slower pace. It was expected that this would be conditional on the type of urban economy. Cities with the highest share of employment in the advanced producer services yield a higher labour demand for less-educated urbanites than those with the lowest share of employment in the advanced producer services. The substitution mechanism between immigrants on the one hand and less-educated natives and former waves of immigrants on the other was thus expected to be stronger in the latter cities than in the former. Put differently, in accordance with the supply-and-demand logic of the substitution thesis, immigration was expected to lead to the most substitution in cities where demand at the bottom of the labour market is lowest. This expectation essentially proved to be correct; immigration did increase the likelihood of unemployment for less-educated urbanites, although this was most significant in cities with the lowest share of employment in the advanced producer services. Meanwhile, in cities with the highest share of this type of employment, the job opportunities for less-educated urbanites were unaffected by immigration.

This finding indicates that it can be very fruitful to look beyond one's own field of inquiry when it comes to solving theoretical puzzles. Many scholars in the field of labour economics often wonder why the impact of immigration on wages and unemployment is less than one might assume on the basis of the theoretical rationale of the substitution thesis (cf. Card, 2005). The insights gained in this study might provide the key explanation. Urban or regional economies differ in the extent to which they are able to absorb immigrants on the labour market. Modelling these differences in future research on the tenability of the substitution thesis might therefore reveal that the weak substitution effects found in previous studies of the theory are the result of the false assumption that cities and regions do not differ in terms of labour demand and/or the supposition that the settlement of immigrants is totally determined by labour market considerations.

6.3 The new conceptual architecture reconsidered

After discussing the findings and their theoretical and empirical implications in the previous sections, it is now time to draw up the balance. The primary aim of this study was to assess whether the central theoretical notions in the global city theoretical framework and debate help us to understand the impact of the current phase of economic globalization on the social and economic realities of cities. The theoretical notions in the global city theoretical framework were formulated because the current phase of economic globalization required a new conceptual architecture (Sassen, 2001: xviii), as the old concepts by which 'sociologists have tended to study cities (...) are no longer sufficient' (Sassen, 1994: xiii). However, the empirical chapters clearly indicated that this new conceptual architecture has substantial flaws and limited merit.

What proved to be most problematic is the assumption that deindustrialization and the clustering of advanced producer services are driven by international outsourcing, especially when combined with the inaccurate supposition in the global city debate that global cities display the future guise of other cities. This is because the former assumption, especially when combined with the latter, has led to a crude overestimation of the impact of economic globalization on urban labour markets. International outsourcing drives deindustrialization and the increase in employment in the advanced producer services in cities in the advanced economies to a very marginal extent. Only the professionals employed in the services that produce the capabilities to manage globally dispersed production processes, i.e. part of the advanced producer services in global cities, can be linked to economic globalization. Many studies in the global city debate therefore falsely attribute the changes in urban labour demand that are driven by deindustrialization and the clustering of advanced producer services to economic globalization on false grounds.

Although the global city theoretical framework and the debate it initiated can be distinguished analytically, in this case they merge empirically. In a recent publication, the architect of the global city theoretical framework used the share of employment in the advanced producer services – a 'globalization variable' (Zhong, Clark & Sassen, 2007: 387) – to assess the impact of economic globalization on more than 250 urban labour markets in the United States. It goes without saying that most of those cities function as, at best, regional nodes or are former industrial strongholds. So, although it cannot be determined from her earlier publications whether Sassen considers the clustering of advanced producer services outside global cities, i.e. in regional nodes and former industrial strongholds, to be the result of international outsourcing, this recent study in the global city debate clearly indicates that she does.

What makes the false assumption that deindustrialization and the clustering of advanced producer services are driven by international outsourcing in all cities in the advanced economies so problematic is the architecture of the global city theoretical framework and the way it has predominantly been used in the global city debate. As this architecture concerns a mix of theories, propositions, and expectations that all build on these false assumptions, it becomes a colossus with feet of clay. This is because, due to these inaccurate suppositions, the application of many of the theoretical assertions in this framework, even if proved to hold true empirically, will ultimately lead to the attribution of social phenomena to economic globalization on false grounds. Consider, for instance, that all of the findings in Chapter 3 suggest that the impact of the clustering of advanced producer services on labour demand needs to be understood according to the basic arguments in the polarization thesis. However, the incorrect assumption that the clustering of advanced producer services in all cities in the advanced economies is driven by international outsourcing in the end leads to the inappropriate attribution to economic globalization of a polarized occupational structure and the unemployment rate that accompanies it.

What seems clear, then, is that several theoretical notions in the global city theoretical framework and debate, especially when combined, do not help us to understand the impact of the current phase of economic globalization on the social and economic realities of cities, but instead lead to a crude overestimation of this effect. Yet, paradoxically, the global city theoretical framework also greatly underestimated this impact. Again, this can primarily be attributed to its architecture, as one of its central assumptions produces a blind spot concerning the impact of economic globalization or, to be more precise, concerning the impact of the globalization of labour. This lacuna is consistent with the productivist bias in the global city theoretical framework, which asserts that immigration to the advanced economies is driven by a high labour demand for low-skilled service workers. In a production-driven world, cities with a low demand for low-skilled labour will simply not attract immigrants.

However, we do not live in a completely production-driven world, and the (immigrant) labour supply in some cities consequently outnumbers labour demand. As a result, substitution in the labour market due to immigration exists. In cities with low shares of employment in the advanced producer services, immigration leads to the increasing likelihood of unemployment for less-educated urbanites, be they immigrants or natives. The blind spot in the global city theoretical framework, and consequently in the global city debate, concerning the possibility of this substitution due to immigration thus led to an underestimation of the impact of economic globalization on urban labour markets.

In summary, most central theoretical notions in the global city theoretical framework and debate were not particularly helpful for understanding the impact of the current phase of economic globalization on the social and economic realities of cities. On the one hand, they led to a great overestimation of the impact of international outsourcing on the economic base, occupational change, and unemployment in cities. On the other, they produced a blind spot for labour market substitution due to the globalization of labour. The new conceptual architecture, then, proved to not be very successful in terms of replacing the old concepts that tended to be used by sociologists to study cities. On the contrary, one of these old concepts – labour market substitution due to immigration – succeeded where the global city theoretical framework failed in explaining the impact of economic globalization on the social and economic realities of cities. The only theoretical reasoning in this framework that proved to be unequivocally successful in explaining globalization's impact concerned the pull factor for new immigration: all the available evidence in Chapter 4 suggested that Dutch investment flows into newly-industrializing countries spawn migration flows in precisely the opposite direction.

The results presented in this study make clear that Sassen's new conceptual architecture largely fails to explain the impact of economic globalization on urban labour markets. This is primarily because this framework is a grand composition of theories, propositions, and expectations that make assumptions about each other's empirical validity. As a consequence, the empirical refutation of its basic assumptions leads to this framework tumbling down like a house of cards. This demonstrated that it is highly problematic if a new conceptual framework formulated to explain new social phenomena is not a middle-range theory (Merton, 1959). Although the global city theoretical framework is built by combining a variety of such theories that can be empirically tested, as a whole it clearly is not such a theory. As a result, it can only be empirically valid if *all* the middle-range theories it is comprised of stand firm in the face of empirical testing. This proved not to be the case, and the standard research practice in the global city debate of using the global city theoretical framework as an 'analytical construct that allows one to detect the global as it is filtered through the specifics of a place' (2006c: x) is therefore highly problematic. This is because this practice boils down to interpreting labour market changes on the basis of this framework and subsequently attributing them to economic globalization. However, the empirical chapters in this study demonstrated that this attribution is largely made on false grounds.

It needs to be emphasized here that I am not the only (or the first) author to be highly critical of the global city theoretical framework, as there are two other strands of criticism. However, I am not convinced by these, and will use the rest of this study to explain why this is the case. The first critique was formulated by James W. White (1998) and will be addressed in this section, while the second, which was produced by Michael Peter Smith (1998), will be examined in Section 6.4.

White considers the global city theoretical framework, which he refers to as 'the global city model' or 'the global city-dual city hypothesis', as 'economically reductionist' (1998: 451). This is because it combines reductionist Marxism – 'economic forces dominate everywhere; the mature capitalist states and multinational firms run the world' (457) – and classic economic theory – 'the world is driven by the market, by utility-maximizing, rational enterprises and managers of capital who disregard and override governments, national borders, public interests, and human welfare drives' (ibid.) – with 'modernization theory, especially its emphasis on convergence' (ibid.). As well as being economically reductionist, White renders the global city theoretical framework ethnocentric; more specifically, it bears evidence of 'American, or Anglo-American, ethnocentrism: The world's greatest cities are not all New York or London, not all countries went through a Reaganite or Thatcherite stage of urbanism, and not all states let the capitalist foxes guard the metropolitan chicken coop' (ibid.).

I have no quarrel with White's characterization of the global city theoretical framework outlined above; it is indeed reductionist and Anglo-American ethnocentric. However, I do not see why this is problematic. On the contrary, theory is *by definition* reductionist in that it reduces the complexity of social reality. Nevertheless, the fact that the global city theoretical framework is *economically* reductionist is problematic when it comes to gaining insight into the causes of urban change, as revealed in the empirical chapters. Furthermore, theory is *by definition* ethnocentric in that it is only applicable to a concrete historical and cultural context. The global city theoretical framework should therefore not be discredited in advance. Instead, the questions of whether changes in urban labour markets are (primarily) driven according to the economic logic of a certain theory, and whether this theory has explanatory power beyond Anglo-American cities, are empirical and call for empirical scrutiny. If the economic logic does not stand the test, labour market changes call for other explanations. Moreover, if it does not stand the test beyond Anglo-American cities, its scope needs to be restricted.

However, this is not what White had in mind after his fierce critique of the global city theoretical framework. Instead of scrutinizing the scope of its empirical worth, he suggests a great leap forward as 'there is, unfortunately, no alternative theory at this point that does specify all the causalities and optional paths at work' (White, 1998: 472). What White in short supposes is a model that is so complex (so 'non-reductionist' in his own terms) that it is able to explain practically everything that has happened in urban labour markets all over the world in recent decades. Such a framework would indeed be empirically valid, but would not reduce the complexity of social realities. On the contrary, it would be just as complex as the social reality it aims to explain, which would render it completely useless. This is because such a framework is no theory at all, but a vast data matrix. It reminds me of a short story by Jorge Luis Borges entitled *On Exactitude in Science* (1975), which mockingly refers to an empire where the science of cartography was so precise that the maps produced were of the same scale as the territory they aimed to represent. These maps were certainly empirically valid, but were also quite useless.

6.4 Globalization or neo-liberalization? On science versus politics

Just like James W. White, Michael Peter Smith is highly critical of the global city theoretical framework. The big difference with White's critique, as well as mine for that matter, is that Smith's criticism does not primarily revolve around the scientific implications of this framework, but its alleged political connotations (White, 1998, 2001). In Smith's reading, the global city theoretical framework does not primarily function as a vessel for interpreting the impact of economic globalization on urban labour markets. Instead, in the article entitled *The Global City - Whose Social Construct is it Anyway,* it is accused of being part of 'a contested political project advanced by powerful social forces' (1998: 483). According to Smith, applying the global city theoretical framework in order to uncover the impact of economic globalization on urban labour markets 'naturalizes' the 'neoliberal regime of "global governance" (...) by legitimating the "reality" of global cities as part and parcel of an unstoppable process of economic globalization. Unintentionally, [global city researchers', JvdW] epistemology thus becomes the ontology of global cities' (Smith, 2001: 65).

According to Smith, then, economic globalization is merely 'the most recent historical version of the free-market ideology' (ibid.). If this is correct, this study did not test the empirical validity of theories that aim to explain the impact of economic globalization on urban labour markets, but is instead part of a project that legitimizes neo-liberalism or the neo-liberal world order.[12] I fundamentally disagree with this, and will use the concluding paragraphs of this study to explain why. Ironically, Smith, who certainly does not consider himself to be a social and cultural conservative, seems to go along with the doctrine that 'what is, is right', which is associated with the Catholic view of history and conservative thinkers like Edmund Burke (cf. Himmelfarb, 1949). For instance, Smith wonders why 'none of the world city scholars, who on the basis of their politics would surely oppose global governance on neoliberal principles, seem to have given much thought to the question of whether their research agenda and "objective" findings implicitly provide support for that very project by legitimizing the reality

12 The concepts 'neo-liberal' and 'neo-liberalism' have been used for such a wide range of ideas and policies that it has practically lost its analytical value. This is because a concept that entails everything is impotent in empirical research as it has no discriminatory value. For the sake of argument, I stick to the conceptualization of Michael Peter Smith, which boils down to classic free-market ideology.

of global cities as part and parcel of the objective processes of economic globalization that they are studying' (1998: 487). However, 'what is' and 'what should be' are not the same, and do indeed differ fundamentally.

What is the object of science. To be clear, it seems very naive to believe that there is an objective social reality out there that the social sciences can reveal and explain. By formulating and testing theories, we attribute selective interpretations to the social phenomena around us, which, in the end, simplify a complex reality (cf. Gouldner, 1970). This is inevitable, and scholarly debates thus revolve around the question of which theory is best able to explain a certain social phenomenon and subsequently lead to bad theories being replaced with better ones. *What should be*, on the other hand, depends on one's notion of 'the good life' and is consequently the object of politics. Which goals should be attained, and what policies should be implemented to do this, i.e. what is right, is a political decision, and is not determined by what is. This is not to say that the interpretations of scholars on how the world works are not related to politics, as they can inform opinions and political debates, but that science can never replace politics. In fact, changing what is because many consider it 'not the way it should be' is what politics entails. Consequently, empirical research does not necessarily legitimize the notion of what is. On the contrary, the corroboration of a certain theoretical logic can just as easily be an impetus to change something, because many regard it as unjustified or illegitimate.

By way of an example, I would like to conclude this section by dealing with Smith's allegation that this is not a scientific study with theoretical relevance, but a neo-liberal manifesto in disguise. The example concerns the finding in this research that immigration leads to unemployment in Dutch cities, which is a potentially explosive outcome given the strong politicization of immigration issues in the Netherlands in recent times (De Koster et al., 2013, 2014; De Koster & Van der Waal, 2014). According to Smith, this apparently needs to be interpreted as a legitimization of a free-market logic, as it renders this logic inevitable. However, my finding that immigration leads to unemployment by no means justifies deregulation of the labour market. By assuming that unemployment is universally considered to be a problem that needs to be addressed, which is a political and not a scientific question, deregulation is merely one option among many others. Social democrats, for example, will probably interpret the aforementioned finding as an indication that *more* state intervention and public spending are needed to produce employment for the unemployed, while nationalists will probably interpret it as a sign that immigration should be reduced. Moreover, some nationalists will agree with the (neo-)

liberals, while others will concur with the social democrats on the extent of state intervention in labour markets. Yet, all (neo-)liberals, social democrats, and nationalists who underscore the basic elements of liberal democracy will strongly oppose a complete closing of borders, as a substantial share of immigration is not driven by market forces, but is due to human rights treaties. Indeed, many consider such immigration to be legitimate, even if it could result in unemployment in a completely deregulated labour market.

In summary, the finding in this study that immigration leads to unemployment legitimates neither neo-liberalism nor the implementation of neo-liberal policies. Put differently, it has no political implications in itself, but if unemployment is considered to be a problem that needs to be addressed, this can be done in many different ways. Accordingly, in this study, the finding that immigration leads to substitution in the labour market neither serves the political project of neo-liberalism, nor any other such project for that matter; it merely serves to corroborate the empirical validity of the substitution thesis. Put differently, it has theoretical implications, i.e. implications for the tenability of a theory, which was why it was assessed. The same is true for the other findings in this study; they merely function to corroborate or reject the theoretical notions under scrutiny. The question of whether the corroborated ideas are best able to explain the empirical generalizations they address is, however, empirical. Indeed, I am quite sure that, someday, another researcher will reject these theoretical notions by corroborating theories that are even better able to explain the social phenomena assessed in this study.

Epilogue: The 2008 financial crisis and its aftermath

This study assessed the empirical tenability of theoretical notions that were formulated to explain urban labour market changes in the latest phase of global capitalism, and it did so for the period 1995 to 2008. With the benefit of hindsight, it could be argued that this time span was very well chosen, as it represents the heyday of the type of capitalist production that this study aimed to scrutinize. This kind of production has been conceptualized, characterized, legitimized, and criticized in various ways, and this epilogue is not the place to discuss these interpretations and judgements at length. However, these explanations also have something in common, namely their emphasis on the central role played by finance and the concomitant advanced producer services such as accountancy, consultancies, law firms, and real estate. They also all consider the clustering of these advanced producer services in cities in the advanced economies as an integral, or even central, part of the type of capitalist production that fell into crisis after the bankruptcy of Lehman Brothers in September 2008. This clustering is the pivot upon which everything hinges in the theoretical notions in the global city debate that were scrutinized in this study. Accordingly, the aforementioned financial crisis and its aftermath – which will, for reasons of brevity, from now on be referred to as 'the crisis' – is highly relevant for the central findings of this research.

It was found in this study that Dutch cities diverged in their post-industrial development: the most service-oriented ones experienced stronger employment growth in the advanced producer services than the former industrial strongholds, and this proved to be highly relevant to their economic fortunes. In particular, it was demonstrated that the growth in those services was very beneficial for the labour market opportunities of less-skilled urbanites. Moreover, it was found that former industrial strongholds consequently have to cope with high unemployment rates among their less-educated inhabitants, while the most service-oriented cities do not. It should also be emphasized that this is not a Dutch idiosyncrasy. Indeed, the available evidence indicates that similar patterns can be found in other European countries (Pratschke & Morlicchio, 2012) and the United States (Florida, 2010; Glaeser, 2009). As a consequence, before the 2008 crisis, many urban policy-makers and politicians in the former industrial strongholds considered attracting advanced producer services to be a viable antidote to high unemployment rates among their less-educated citizens. However, the crisis has discredited advanced producer service-driven urban economic growth among politicians, policy-makers, and substantial parts of the population alike.

The reason why this is the case is that, for many, it entails or represents a part of the problem instead of the solution. What is more, as the primary producers and benefiters of the financial products that many consider to be the root cause of the crisis, large parts of the advanced producer services – most notably those revolving around financial services – have been pinpointed as the villains of the piece. Indeed, an example is the chapter title *Fire Starter* in Florida's book, *The Great Reset. How New Ways of Living and Working Drive Post-Crash Prosperity,* which elaborates on the role that the advanced producer services – referred to with the widely-used acronym FIRE (Finance, Insurance, and Real Estate) – have allegedly played in the crisis (2010: 61-5). This clearly and creatively voices a broadly supported analysis of how the crisis came about. Accordingly, pre-crisis urban economic growth driven by the advanced producer services has become discredited in recent years, and is, according to many, certainly not the path to follow in the future. How, then, will urban economies develop in the years to come, and what does this mean for the unequal economic development across cities that has been demonstrated in this study to be the result of economic growth driven by the advanced producer services in the 1990s and 2000s? Three scenarios can be distinguished based on the combination of the findings in this study and reflections on the impact of the crisis on the economic fortunes of cities.

The first scenario is that the city-level differences mentioned above in terms of economic fortunes will wither, because the economic advantage that the most service-oriented cities had will vanish due to the declining salience of the advanced producer services. This would mean that all cities, and not just the former industrial strongholds, would have to cope with high unemployment rates among the less educated in the years to come. I argue that this is the least likely scenario. Even in the case of the declining salience of advanced producer services, the demand for low-skilled service workers will always be higher in the most service-oriented cities, as the activities they need to employ are far more labour intensive than those in manufacturing-like production. Furthermore, as there is no indication or argument that the crisis and its aftermath will be detrimental to the economic gains of the clustering of advanced producer services in certain places, the most service-oriented cities will continue to be the most service-oriented. Accordingly, the declining salience of advanced producer services might reduce the differences in employment opportunities for the low-skilled between service-oriented cities and former industrial strongholds, but these differences will, nevertheless, endure.

According to the second scenario, the divergence between the economic fortunes of service-oriented cities and former industrial strongholds will continue, or even increase, as the former have a more highly-skilled workforce and diversified economy (Glaeser, 2009). As a result, the level of creativity and potential for innovation in service-oriented cities is much higher. New and innovative services and products that can put the economy back on track are, therefore, more likely to be conceptualized and developed in those cities than in former industrial strongholds. Some even argue that this potential for innovation has partly been hampered in recent decades, as many talented, highly-educated young people have opted for a career in finance for pecuniary reasons, instead of utilizing their talents to develop products and services in the so-called 'real economy' (Black, 2009). Indeed, consider Barack Obama's 2009 reflections on the crisis: 'We don't want every single college grad with mathematical aptitude to become a derivatives trader. We want some of them to go into engineering, and we want some of them to be going into computer design' (Leonhardt, 2009). As such, a decline in the salience of finance and related services could even be regarded as a blessing in disguise by those who concur with Obama on this matter, as it will result in a shift of creative labour power to activities that are considered to be more beneficial for sustainable economic growth.

I would like to argue that the second scenario is more likely than the first, although there is one caveat. A highly-skilled, creative, and innovative workforce is undoubtedly beneficial for economic development, but not all such development will be able to alleviate the plight of unemployed less-skilled urbanites, as the notion of 'jobless growth' suggests. Certainly, the types of jobs available for the less-skilled that the clustering of advanced producer services creates are sometimes denounced as 'McJobs' or 'dead-end jobs', with those taking them being pitied as a 'service proletariat'. These characterizations are made with reference to steady, well-paying jobs in manufacturing, but one could also argue that having a job – even a 'dead-end' one – trumps having no job at all as a result of production in manufacturing being automated or outsourced. As a scholar, it is not up to me to decide what is good or bad, because the answer to the question of which option is good in a normative sense cannot be determined by scientific means. Nevertheless, I would like to point out that the future economic activities that will be developed and used in cities by the highly-skilled, and which might be very beneficial for economic growth, will not by definition result in a high labour demand for the less educated. The pre-crisis growth model did accord with Sassen's polarization thesis, as has been demonstrated in this study. However, whether the future endeavours of the highly-educated workforce will be as beneficial for the employment opportunities of less-educated urbanites is still an open question.

The third and final scenario for post-crisis urban labour markets that I would like to address has explicitly been formulated in reaction to the pre-crisis urban-growth model (Florida, 2010; Indergaard et al., 2013). The title of a recent special issue of *Cities*, which elaborated on this scenario, speaks volumes: *Creative Cities after the Fall of Finance* (Indergaard et al., 2013). Indeed, according to its proponents, this scenario already hints at the potential cure – creativity – for the economic downturn that FIRE started. As such, it is related to the second scenario, although there is one crucial difference: whereas the second scenario starts with the empirical observation that service-oriented cities harbour a highly-educated workforce and are therefore more likely to get back on track than their industrial counterparts, the third version revolves around creating a culturally stimulating environment where artists and cultural industries can thrive. This can be achieved in different ways, and is considered to be beneficial for economic development for a number of reasons (Grodach, 2013), among which is the attraction of a creative workforce, as theorized by Florida, and as addressed in Chapter 3 of this book. Furthermore, various studies on both sides of the Atlantic indicate that cities that are rich in cultural amenities do indeed attract people in creative occupations and thrive economically (e.g. Currid, 2009; Currid-Halkett & Stolarick, 2013; Florida et al., 2008; Wojan et al., 2007). This gives the third post-crisis scenario some empirical basis.

Yet, Chapter 3 demonstrated that the presence of cultural industries could not explain the varying unemployment rates among the less educated across Dutch cities, while the presence of advanced producer services could. This suggests that the previously established cultural industry-driven urban economic growth will not automatically translate into a high labour demand for less-educated urbanites, unlike urban economic growth driven by the advanced producer services. However, as emphasized in Chapter 3, Dutch peculiarities – small inter-city distances in an extended welfare state, and a state-subsidized cultural sector – might be responsible for the finding that the cultural industries do not affect the unemployment rates of the less educated. If this is correct, it may be that the cultural industries do yield a demand for low-skilled service workers in the Netherlands, although this demand is less place-bound and place-specific than in more economically deregulated and vast countries such as the United States. For cities in the latter type of country, the cultural industries might, thus, be a viable post-crisis option for economic growth that will also be beneficial for the employment opportunities of less-educated urbanites.

If this is accurate, the question remains whether this scenario will aggravate or diminish the differences in employment opportunities between service-oriented cities and more industrial ones in such countries. The answer to that question depends on the extent to which former industrial strongholds are able to market their cultural heritage and employ new cultural activities that can attract higher-educated and creative people. On the one hand, this and other studies have demonstrated that cultural industries can particularly be found in the most service-oriented cities, which indicates that the third post-crisis scenario will aggravate the difference in unemployment rates between such cities and former industrial strongholds. On the other hand, several individual cases like Chicago and Bilbao indicate that cities can overcome the shadow that their industrial legacy casts on their current and future economic fortunes. As such, the third post-crisis scenario is the only one that gives urban policy-makers some guidance on how to escape the current economic downturn if the pre-crisis urban economic growth model has permanently fallen from grace. Time will, however, tell whether the pre-crisis growth model will indeed be replaced and, if so, whether this will be in accordance with one of the scenarios theorized here.

Appendix A Polarization and professionalization studies

Table A1 contains all the studies known to the author that assess whether the occupational and/or income hierarchy in cities polarizes or professionalizes *on the basis of the polarization thesis in the global city theoretical framework and/or Hamnett's professionalization thesis.* Several studies that are informed by these theories are omitted from the table, because the findings cannot be directly or indirectly categorized according to this scheme. Not included, for instance, are studies that assess income inequality measured as the difference between the poorest and richest urbanites (e.g. with Gini-coefficients), instead of the absolute or relative growth of income categories.

Table A1 Empirical studies on the occupational and income hierarchy in cities informed by the polarization and professionalization thesis

Authors	City/cities	Dependents	Findings
Baum, 1997	Sydney	Occupations & income	Occupational & income polarization
Baum, 1999	Singapore	Occupations & income	Occupational & income professionalization
Beer & Forster, 2002			
Borel-Saladin & Crankshaw, 2009	Cape town	Occupations	Professionalization
Brint, 1991	New York	Occupations	Professionalization
Burgers, 1996	Amsterdam, Rotterdam, The Hague, Utrecht	Employment	Professionalization
Burgers & Musterd, 2002	Amsterdam, Rotterdam	Occupations	Polarization (Amsterdam), professionalization (Rotterdam)
Chiu & Lui, 2004	Hong Kong	Occupations & income	Occupational & income polarization
Cox & Watt, 2002	London	Informal employment	Growth informal domestic labour
Crankshaw, 2012	Cape Town	Occupations & unemployment	Professionalization
Crankshaw & Borel-Saladin, 2014	Johannesburg	Occupations & income	Occupational & income professionalization
Elliott, 1999a, 199b, 2004	105 US metropolitan areas	Low-wage employment	Least low-income employment in the most global cities
Gordon & Sassen, 1992	London	Income	Polarization
Hamnett,1994a	Amsterdam, Rotterdam, The Hague, Utrecht	Occupations	Professionalization
Hamnett, 1994b	London	Occupations	Professionalization
Hamnett, 1996a	London	Occupations & income	Occupational professionalization & income polarization
Hamnett & Cross, 1998	London	Income	Polarization
Hamnett, 2004	London	Occupations & income	Occupational & income professionalization
Kloosterman, 1996	Amsterdam, Rotterdam	Occupations & income	Occupational & income polarization

Authors	City/cities	Dependents	Findings
Lemanski, 2007	Cape Town	Occupations & income	Occupational & income polarization
Ley, 1996	Halifax, Montreal, Ottawa, Toronto Edmonton, Vancouver	Occupations	Professionalization
MacLachlan & Sawada, 1997	22 Canadian metropolitan areas	Income	Polarization
Maloutas, 2007	Athens	Occupations	Polarization
May et al., 2007	London	Occupations	Polarization
Norgaard, 2003	New York	Income	Polarization
Rhein, 1996	Paris	Occupations	Professionalization
Tai, 2006	Singapore, Hong Kong, Taipei	Occupations	Polarization (Singapore, Hong Kong), polarization (Taipei)
Tai, 2010	Singapore, Hong Kong, Taipei, Seoul	Occupations	Professionalization
Timberlake et al., 2012	100 US metropolitan areas	Income	Professionalization
Van der Waal & Burgers, 2010	Amsterdam, Rotterdam	Income	Polarization
Walks, 2001	Toronto	Occupations & income	Occupational professionalization & income polarization
Wessel, 2001	Oslo	Income	Polarization
Zhong et al., 2007	257 US metropolitan areas	Income	No polarization

Appendix B Data & operationalization

For the analyses in Chapters 2, 3, and 5 on the 22 Dutch metropolitan areas (see map B1 for their delineations), I have constructed my own dataset with data I was able to retrieve via the StatLine service of Statistics Netherlands (*Centraal Bureau voor de Statistiek, CBS*).[13] The dataset contains information on employment shares by industry, unemployment rates, immigrant shares, and relevant demographic characteristics for these areas. The maximum range of years goes from 1995 to 2007. Nevertheless, some variables were not available for this full period. Unfortunately, information on employment shares by industry from 2008 onwards cannot be compared to those shares up to 2008, due to differences in the measurement of economic activities. As a result, the most recent data that can be utilized for assessing both trends in employment shares in industries (Chapter 2), and the impact of those shares on unemployment (Chapters 3 and 5), relate to 2007.

The operationalization of the variables will be outlined below, and they are categorized according to the first chapter in which they appear. The descriptives of the variables can be found in Table B1.

Table B1 Descriptives of variables in the dataset on labour market indicators for the 22 Dutch metropolitan areas

Variable	Minimum share	Maximum share	Mean share	Standard deviation	Data range	N
Age 15-24	6.67	21.21	11.58	2.14	1995-2007	286
Cultural industries	2.03	6.67	3.82	1.06	1995-2007	286
Hotel and catering industry	1.40	5.52	3.07	0.76	1995-2007	286
Immigrant share	7.69	39.13	19.18	5.89	1996-2007	264
Manufacturing	4.00	31.80	12.45	5.08	1995-2007	286
Advanced producer services	12.00	33.57	21.35	4.82	1995-2007	286
Unemployment rate	2.00	16.20	6.21	2.34	1996-2007	264
Unemployment rate less educated	0.10	12.30	4.62	1.85	1996-2007	264
Working population	33.00	486.00	118.74	108.10	1995-2007	286

Source: StatLine CBS (own calculations)

13 http://statline.cbs.nl/statweb/

Map B1 The 22 Dutch metropolitan areas (source: Vliegen, 2005)

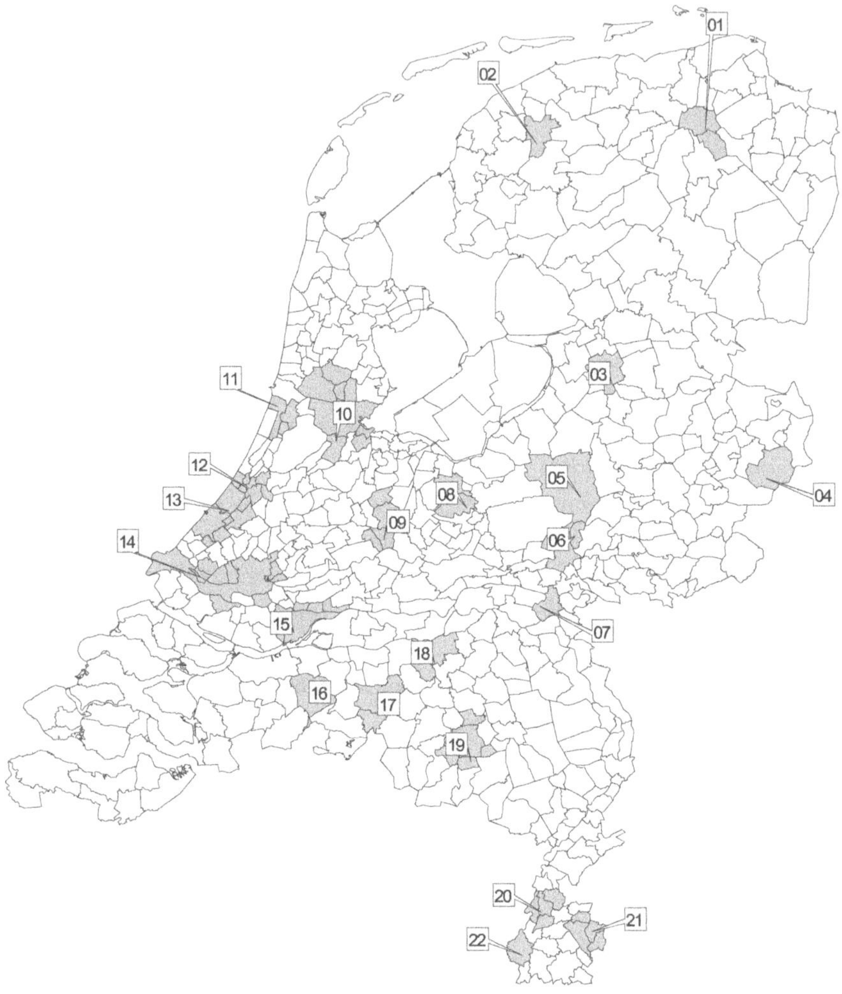

1	Groningen	9	Utrecht	17	Tilburg
2	Leeuwarden	10	Amsterdam	18	's Hertogenbosch
3	Zwolle	11	Haarlem	19	Eindhoven
4	Enschede	12	Leiden	20	Sittard-Geleen
5	Apeldoorn	13	The Hague	21	Heerlen
6	Arnhem	14	Rotterdam	22	Maastricht
7	Nijmegen	15	Dordrecht		
8	Amersfoort	16	Breda		

Variables introduced in Chapter 2

Manufacturing – concerns the share of employment in the manufacturing industry. It is measured as the share of the working population that is employed in firms classified in Class D in the Dutch SBI 93 classification scheme (*Standaard Bedrijfsindeling 1993*). This scheme corresponds to the 'ISIC Rev. 3.1' (International Standard Industrial Classification of All Economic Activities) of the United Nations (*data range* 1995-2007).

Producer services – concerns the share of the working population that is employed in firms classified in Class J (finance) and Class K (real estate and producer services) in the Dutch SBI 93 classification scheme (*data range* 1995-2007).

Variables introduced in Chapter 3

Age 15-24 – concerns a variable that measures the share of the working population in the age category 15 to 24. It is used to control for non-labour market driven settlement patterns, such as the high share of students in university cities (*data range* 1995-2007).

Cultural industries – concerns the share of the working population that is employed in firms classified in Class O (recreational, cultural, and sporting activities) in the Dutch SBI 93 classification scheme. Accordingly, it indicates the extent to which an urban economy functions as an entertainment machine. It must be noted, however, that the category *cultural industries* is assessed with a rather crude measure for the issue at hand, as it also covers the production of cultural goods directed at the non-local market. There is, nevertheless, unfortunately no less-crude measure of cultural production available at the city level (*data range* 1995-2007).

Hotel and catering industry – concerns the share of the working population that is employed in firms classified in Class H (hotels and restaurants) in the Dutch SBI 93 classification scheme (*data range* 1995-2007).

Unemployment rate less educated – measures the share of the less-educated working population that is currently unemployed, but looking for a job for at least 12 hours a week (*data range* 1995-2007). Those that fall within categories 1 and 2 of the International Standard Classification of Education (ISCED) are considered to be less educated. *Unemployment rate less educated* is calculated by subtracting the employed less-educated working population from the total less-educated working population. In the Netherlands, the total working population is measured as those employed, plus those who are currently looking for a job for at least 12 hours a week (*data range* 1996-2007).

Unemployment – measures the share of the total working population that is currently unemployed, but is looking for a job for at least 12 hours a week (*data range* 1995-2007). It is used to ensure the robustness of the findings of the analyses on the *unemployment rate less educated* (see Appendix D), as the calculation of the latter measure did yield a remarkably low minimum score (*data range* 1996-2007).

Working population – measures the total number of urbanites between the ages of 15 and 66. As such, it indicates the total working population. This variable is entered into the analyses in logarithmic form due to its skewed distribution (*data range* 1995-2007).

Variables introduced in Chapter 4

To assess the impact of Dutch foreign direct investments on new migration flows to the 22 Dutch metropolitan areas, I had to combine data retrieved from the StatLine service of Statistics Netherlands on immigration flows to Dutch cities with data from UNCTAD, the World Bank, and the Immigration and Naturalization Service (*Immigratie- en Naturalisatiedienst, IND*). The data from Statistics Netherlands concern the increase in the number of immigrants in each Dutch metropolitan area by country of origin between 1996 and 2009.

The assessment of the pull factor explanation, of course, calls for a comparison of cities instead of immigrant-sending countries, and therefore compares the 22 Dutch metropolitan areas. All variables are outlined below in the order they appear in the analyses.

Variables in the push factor analysis

Growth immigrant groups – measures the increase in the number of immigrants in Amsterdam (*growth in immigrants Amsterdam*) and the 22 Dutch metropolitan areas combined (*growth in immigrants Dutch cities*) from non-European, non-OECD countries by country of origin between 1996 and 2010.[14] Unlike Ricketts (1987), I measured the absolute increase in immigrant groups instead of the relative increase, i.e. total growth instead of growth relative to the population size of the sending country. This is because the argument addressed in this book revolves around the absolute number of people uprooted by investments, not the relative number.

Table B2 presents 1) the number of all documented immigrants from non-OECD countries outside Europe by country of origin in 1996 and 2009, and 2) the growth in that number between those years for both Amsterdam

14 Former Eastern Bloc countries are left out of the analyses, as these countries (mostly) joined the European Union, and some the OECD, in the assessed period. This was accompanied by another regulatory regime for the movement of labour. Consequently, it is impossible to disentangle empirically the extent to which immigration from these countries to the Netherlands is driven by Dutch FDI or the regime change.

Table B2 Number of immigrants from non-OECD countries outside Europe by country of origin in Amsterdam and the 22 Dutch metropolitan areas combined in 1996 and 2009, and the growth in this number between 1996 and 2009

	Amsterdam			22 Dutch metropolitan areas		
	1996	*2009*	*Δ1996-2009*	*1996*	*2009*	*Δ1996-2009*
Afghanistan	344	1964	1620	1445	10,885	9440
Brazil	868	1836	968	2345	5469	3124
Cape Verde	357	314	-43	9167	9382	215
China	1504	2854	1350	7455	19,117	11,662
Colombia	590	1257	667	2593	5324	2731
Dominican	1170	1462	292	3041	4822	1781
Dutch Antilles	7398	7370	-28	35,895	49,351	13,456
Egypt	2588	3452	864	4979	6629	1650
Ethiopia	1052	1136	84	3771	4434	663
Ghana	5255	6688	1433	7872	9583	1711
Hong Kong	1476	1354	-122	5706	5573	-133
India	1916	3121	1205	4957	9109	4152
Indonesia	11,621	8951	-2670	64,747	51,464	-13,283
Iran	1396	1999	603	6667	11,183	4516
Iraq	882	1911	1029	3702	13,763	10,061
Morocco	29,635	34,184	4549	90,617	105,679	15,062
Pakistan	3205	3225	20	7648	7897	249
Philippines	997	1371	374	2403	4167	1764
Russian Federation	1025	3236	2211	3598	15,975	12,377
Somalia	578	703	125	5640	6256	616
Surinam	45,680	39,902	-5778	126,282	118,803	-7479
Vietnam	110	271	161	2680	3833	1153
Total	119,647	128,561	8914	403,210	478,698	75,488

Source: StatLine CBS (own calculations)

and the 22 Dutch metropolitan areas combined. Three countries – former colonies – are excluded from the regression analyses in Chapter 4: the Dutch Antilles, Indonesia, and Surinam. Many of the immigrants from these areas – the first of which is still part of the Kingdom of the Netherlands – hold Dutch citizenship. Furthermore, and more importantly here, the bulk of the people living there are familiar with the Netherlands and Dutch culture due to previous colonial ties. Accordingly, there is a need to empirically disentangle the effect of cultural ties stemming from (previous) colonial bonds between (the European part of) the Netherlands and Indonesia, Surinam, and the Dutch Antilles from the cultural ties between the Netherlands and those three countries that are the result from Dutch investments. Unfortunately, the quantitative approach used in this study does not allow the disentangling of the two types of cultural ties mentioned above in any other way than by simply removing these countries from the analyses.

Of course, the immigrant influx in Dutch cities from the 19 countries that remain can also have causes, such as political reasons and chain migration, other than the FDI-migration nexus that is the main focus of Chapter 4. However, as we will see below, these causes can be controlled for in the analyses.

Unfortunately, the data used do not allow immigrants to be selected by their education level, while the push and pull factor explanations addressed in Chapter 4 obviously revolve around the migration of less-educated immigrants. The analyses will therefore be performed while controlling for the estimated share of so-called 'knowledge workers' in each immigrant group.[15] Furthermore, one country of origin in the dataset – Morocco – has been sending 'guest workers' to the Netherlands from the 1960s onwards. Although the recruitment of guest workers stopped in the 1980s, the Netherlands has experienced a substantial influx of Moroccans ever since. For a large part, that influx is the result of so-called 'family migration', i.e. the reunification or formation of families. In the period under scrutiny (1996-2009), no less than 87% of the immigrant influx from Morocco involved such family migration (own calculations using data from StatLine Statistics Netherlands). Consequently, the increase in immigrants from Morocco shown in Table B2 is reduced by 87% in the regression analyses in Chapter 4.

15 Since 2004, the IND has registered the number of knowledge workers who applied for residence in the Netherlands (INDIAC, 2009). Its figures indicate that from the nineteen countries in the dataset, three did send a substantial number of such immigrants: India, China, and Russia. The average annual numbers of knowledge workers from these countries between 2005 and 2009 are used as proxies for the percentage of the total increase in immigrants from those countries in that period. This would mean that 11.8% of the Russian, 27.8% of the Chinese, and 128% of the Indian immigrants in the dataset were knowledge workers between 2005 and 2009. These percentages are used as an indicator of the share of knowledge workers from these countries in the complete time period assessed in Chapter 4 (1996-2009). The growth in the number of Russian, Chinese, and Indian immigrants has therefore been reduced by 11.8%, 27.8%, and 100% in the analyses, respectively. The number of knowledge workers from India in the Netherlands as a whole exceeds the total number of Indian immigrants who settled in the 22 Dutch metropolitan areas combined in the assessed time period. This indicates that the number of knowledge workers is overestimated in the analyses, and means that the FDI-immigration nexus is tested very strictly.

Of course, guest worker recruitment schemes did result in cultural ties between Morocco and the Netherlands that are more encompassing than the nuclear family ties of those who were recruited. Nevertheless, the impact of these more demographically-encompassing ties are controlled for, as the analyses that follow also model so-called 'chain migration' (see below) (data: *CBS* and *IND*).

Growth Dutch FDI – measures the increase in FDI stock stemming from the Netherlands in the immigrant-sending countries in the period 1993-2006. The FDI stock has thus been measured with a time lag of three years prior to the *growth in immigrant groups*, as the migration effects of foreign direct investments are unlikely to occur instantly; modelling a time lag is therefore standard research practice in this kind of analysis. Instead of the *relative* growth in the period under scrutiny (cf. Ricketts, 1987; Sanderson & Kentor, 2008; Yang, 1998), I used the *absolute* growth, i.e. the total amount instead of the percentage of the gross domestic product of the receiving country. This is most in accordance with the theoretical rationale addressed in Chapter 4, i.e. the absolute amount is a more accurate measure of the number of people employed in FDI-financed production sites/export processing zones than the relative amount. These are the people that are likely to be 'pushed' towards migration. *Growth in Dutch FDI* proved to be strongly skewed (it had a skewness score of more than 2), and its logarithmic form is therefore used in the analyses (data: UNCTAD).

Growth total FDI – measures, in a similar way to *Growth Dutch FDI*, the increase in total FDI stock in the immigrant-sending countries in the period 1993-2006. It is used to empirically disentangle the 'long recognized westernization effect of large-scale foreign investment' (Sassen, 1988: 18-9) from the effects induced by the cultural links stemming from the Dutch FDI. It is, after all, the latter that we are interested in for explaining migration flows to Dutch cities, while the former might also be responsible for (part of) that migration. *Growth total FDI* is strongly skewed (its skewness score is above 2), and its logarithmic form is therefore used in the analyses (data: UNCTAD).

Population growth – is the first indicator used to control for classic migration theories. It is measured as the population growth in the immigrant-sending countries between 1999 and 2000 as a percentage of the population in 1999 (data: World Bank).

Gross domestic product per capita – is the second indicator used to control for classic migration theories. It measures the gross domestic product of the immigrant-sending countries in the year 2000 divided by their population size (data: World Bank).

Distance – for a proper test of both the FDI-migration nexus and the classic migration theories, there is a need for control variables. The first of these measures the distance between the immigrant-sending country and the Netherlands, as it is expected that long distances will hamper migration (cf. Portes, 2000) (data: www.timeanddate.com/).

Asylum requests – is the second control variable. Various immigrant-sending countries experienced political turmoil during the period assessed in Chapter 4, most notably Afghanistan, Iran, Iraq, and Somalia. Consequently, part of the immigrant influx from those countries involves refugees who have been granted access to the Netherlands on the basis of human rights treaties. To empirically disentangle such immigration from that stemming from FDI investments and/or population pressures and underdevelopment, the analyses control for the number of asylum requests the Netherlands received from all countries in the dataset in the period under scrutiny (data: *CBS*).

Immigrants 1996 – to control for chain migration (Portes, 2000), the third control variable measures the number of immigrants from each country in the first year of the assessed time period in Amsterdam (*immigrants 1996 Amsterdam*) and the 22 Dutch metropolitan areas combined (*immigrants 1996 Dutch cities*). Both measures had a skewness score of more than 2, and are therefore entered in the analyses in logarithmic form (data: *CBS*).

Variables in the pull factor analysis

Growth immigrant share – measures the increase in the immigrant population between 1997 and 2008 in the 22 Dutch metropolitan areas as the share of the working population in 1997. This increase has been measured while also controlling for the number of knowledge workers and family migration from Morocco (compare the measurement of *growth immigrant groups* for the push factor analysis). *Growth immigrant share* has a slightly smaller data range than the one used when assessing the push factor explanation. This is because the data for the pull factor could not be retrieved for such a wide range of years (see below) (data: *CBS*).

Growth employment advanced producer services – measures the growth in the share of the working population in each agglomeration that is employed in firms classified in Class J (finance) and Class K (real estate and producer services) in the International Standard Industrial Classification of All Economic Activities scheme of the United Nations (ISIC Rev. 3.1). The maximum data range that could be retrieved ranges from 1995 to 2008. As such, it measures the employment growth two years prior to the growth in the immigrant share in the working population. Such a two-year time lag is standard research practice in labour market studies, because the migration effects of labour demand are unlikely to occur instantly (data: *CBS*).

Growth employment hotel and catering industry – measures the growth in the share of the working population that is employed in firms classified in Class H in the ISIC Rev. 3.1 classification between 1995 and 2008. For similar reasons, like *growth employment advanced producer services* it is measured with a two-year time lag.

Immigrants 1997 – measures the share of immigrants in the working population of each metropolitan area in 1997. It is used as a control variable for chain migration (Portes, 2000) and the notion that the consumption of low-wage immigrants in itself spawns a demand for labour that attracts new waves of immigration (Sassen-Koob, 1984b, 1986; Sassen, 1993) (data: *CBS*).

Variables introduced in Chapter 5

The dataset used in Chapter 5 is the same one utilized in Chapters 2 and 3 on the 22 Dutch metropolitan areas, with one additional variable, *immigrant share*, which measures the share of immigrants in the working population (*data range* 1996-2007).

Appendix C Employment shares in manufacturing for each metropolitan area 1995-2007

Table C1 Employment shares in manufacturing in the 22 Dutch metropolitan areas (1995-2007)

	1995	1996	1997	1998	1999	2000	2001	2002	2003	2004	2005	2006	2007	Δ (1995-2007)
Amersfoort	10.0	10.0	10.0	9.0	9.2	8.6	8.0	7.9	7.5	7.4	6.9	6.8	6.5	3.5
Amsterdam	9.9	9.3	9.0	8.4	8.2	7.7	7.2	6.8	6.6	6.3	6.1	6.0	6.0	3.9
Apeldoorn	15.3	14.5	14.8	13.8	13.1	12.8	12.7	12.4	12.1	11.2	11.2	10.0	10.0	5.3
Arnhem	9.0	9.0	9.0	8.0	7.7	7.6	8.0	8.0	7.0	7.0	7.0	7.0	7.0	2.0
Breda	16.3	15.7	14.6	14.1	13.7	13.0	13.3	13.0	12.6	12.1	11.7	10.7	10.3	6.0
Den Bosch	15.0	13.6	12.6	12.0	11.8	12.2	11.3	10.8	9.5	8.1	7.4	7.2	7.0	8.0
Dordrecht	20.2	19.5	17.9	17.3	16.3	15.0	15.0	14.0	14.0	14.0	13.0	13.0	13.0	7.2
Eindhoven	26.0	26.2	24.9	24.9	23.6	21.8	21.6	21.5	21.2	20.2	19.7	18.7	18.4	7.6
Enschede	19.7	18.5	17.7	17.5	17.5	17.0	16.7	16.5	16.1	15.5	15.7	14.9	14.3	5.4
Groningen	9.8	9.4	9.3	8.7	8.6	8.3	8.1	7.8	7.4	6.8	6.6	6.8	6.5	3.3
Haarlem	14.2	13.1	11.9	11.7	10.6	10.3	10.8	11.6	10.2	9.3	8.5	9.0	9.0	5.2
Heerlen	22.8	21.8	20.3	20.0	19.2	18.3	17.8	18.1	16.9	16.3	15.0	14.9	14.1	8.7
Leeuwarden	12.3	11.0	11.3	10.8	9.8	9.0	9.2	8.6	8.7	8.5	8.4	7.7	7.3	5.0
Leiden	8.9	9.0	9.1	9.1	9.1	8.0	8.0	8.0	8.0	8.0	8.0	8.0	8.0	0.9
Maastricht	20.9	19.6	18.3	17.7	16.8	16.0	15.0	14.0	13.0	12.0	12.0	11.4	11.4	9.5
Nijmegen	17.0	17.0	17.0	17.0	17.0	16.0	16.0	16.0	16.0	16.0	16.0	16.0	16.0	1.0
Rotterdam	13.1	12.8	12.2	11.7	11.3	10.9	9.9	10.0	10.0	9.0	9.0	8.9	8.5	4.6
Sittard-Geleen	31.8	25.4	23.4	22.0	22.0	21.0	20.0	21.0	21.0	22.0	23.0	24.7	23.4	8.4
The Hague	8.0	8.0	8.0	8.0	7.0	7.0	7.0	7.0	7.0	7.0	7.0	7.0	7.0	1.0
Tilburg	19.0	18.7	17.5	17.0	17.2	17.7	18.4	18.1	17.2	15.8	15.1	15.0	15.0	4.0
Utrecht	7.3	7.1	6.3	6.2	5.8	6.3	6.1	5.0	5.0	5.0	5.0	5.0	4.0	3.3
Zwolle	12.1	12.1	11.0	11.0	11.0	10.0	10.0	10.0	10.0	9.0	9.0	8.1	8.1	3.0

Source: StatLine CBS (own calculations)

Appendix D Robustness checks

As outlined in Appendix B, the calculation of *unemployment rate less educated* resulted in a remarkable finding: the lowest score of that variable was close to zero (0.1%). In reality, such a low unemployment rate among the less educated will never occur. Moreover, the highest score on *unemployment rate less educated* is lower than the highest score on *unemployment rate* (12.30 < 16.20, see Table B1). This is also very unlikely, as the unemployment rate among the least skilled is always higher than among the most skilled. Both of the above-mentioned peculiarities of *unemployment rate less educated* indicate that it underestimates the very employment level it aims to measure. This is why all of the analyses on that variable in Chapters 3 and

Table D1 Zero-order correlations of unemployment rate with unemployment rate less educated for all 22 Dutch metropolitan areas (1996-2007)

	Zero-order correlation	*N* (number of years)
Amersfoort	0.90***	12
Amsterdam	0.95***	12
Apeldoorn	0.77**	12
Arnhem	0.78**	12
Breda	0.90***	12
Den Bosch	0.80**	12
Dordrecht	0.93***	12
Eindhoven	0.87***	12
Enschede	0.82**	12
Groningen	0.81**	12
Haarlem	0.52	12
Heerlen	0.89***	12
Leeuwarden	0.68*	12
Leiden	0.82**	12
Maastricht	0.96***	12
Nijmegen	0.82**	12
Rotterdam	0.97***	12
Sittard-Geleen	0.93***	12
The Hague	0.80**	12
Tilburg	0.83**	12
Utrecht	0.78**	12
Zwolle	0.77**	12

Source: StatLine CBS (own calculations)
$^{*}p < 0.05$; $^{**}p < 0.01$; $^{***}p < 0.001$

5 are replicated in this appendix with analyses on the most conceptually and empirically closely-related indicator: the general unemployment rate (from now on referred to as *unemployment rate*).

Unemployment rate and *unemployment rate less educated* are very highly correlated (see Table D1), which suggests that the latter is particularly reliable as an indicator of the differences in unemployment rates of the less educated across years and cities. As previously noted, it merely underestimates that level; however, as the findings in Table D1 indicate, it does so consistently across all years and cities.

Robustness checks on the findings in Table 3.1

Table D2 replicates the analysis in Table 3.1 on the impact of the producer services on the unemployment rate of less-educated urbanites, and yields similar results. Just like Table 3.1, it indicates that in cities with the highest employment shares in the advanced producer services, the unemployment rate is the lowest, as predicted on the basis of the polarization thesis. Consequently, Figure D1 is very similar to Figure 3.1, although the predicted unemployment rates are higher in the former than in the latter. This is in line with the previously mentioned underestimation of the unemployment rate among the less educated by *unemployment rate less educated*.

Table D2 also indicates that the effect of the employment shares in the advanced producer services is not (partly) driven by the employment shares

Table D2 Unemployment rate in the 22 Dutch metropolitan areas (1996-2007), explained by the employment shares in the advanced producer services and the hotel and catering industry (multilevel regression analysis; entries are regression coefficients; estimation: maximum likelihood)

	Null model	Model 1	Model 2
Independents	*B*	*B*	*B*
Constant	6.21***	16.53***	16.77**
Advanced producer services		-0.38***	-0.37***
Hotel and catering industry			-0.11
Controls			
Age 15-24		-0.18**	-0.18**
Variance metropolitan level ($N = 22$)	1.48	2.38	2.37
Variance year level ($N = 12$)	1.80	1.61	1.61
Log likelihood	-554.15	-536.52	-536.45

Source: StatLine CBS (own calculations)
*$p < 0.05$; **$p < 0.01$; ***$p < 0.001$

in the hotel and catering industry, which is also in accordance with the analysis in Table 3.1. Overall, Table D2 and Figure D1 clearly indicate that the findings in Table 3.1 are robust.

Figure D1 Unemployment rate of urbanites as predicted by the employment shares in advanced producer services in the 22 Dutch metropolitan areas

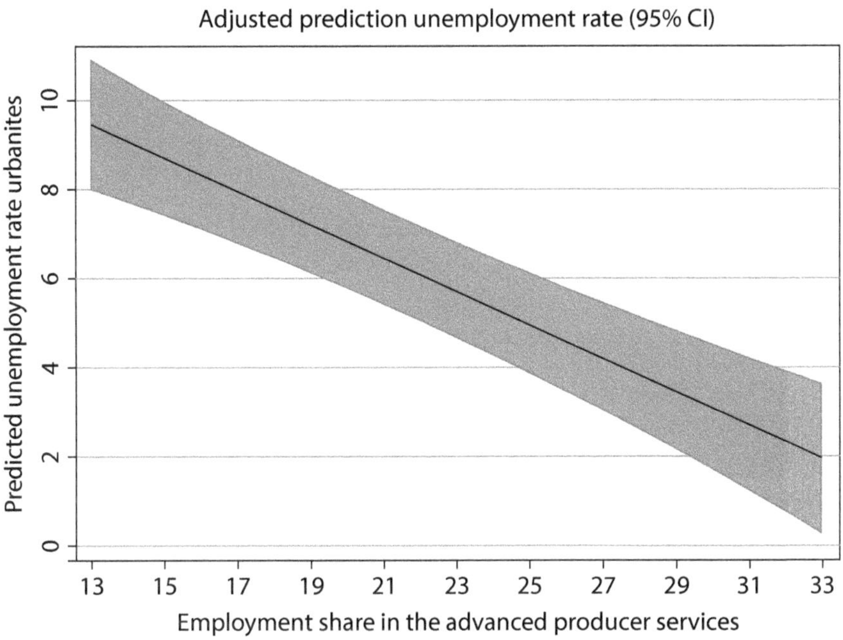

Robustness checks on the findings in Table 3.3

The robustness check of the results in the analysis presented in Table 3.3 can be found in Table D3 below. Model 1 depicts the findings already presented in Model 2 of Table D2, while Model 2 depicts the robustness check of the central finding of Table 3.4, i.e. that the cultural industries do not negatively affect the unemployment rates of less-educated urbanites, as consumerist theorizing predicts. The latter model replicates that finding for *unemployment rate*. Just like Model 2 in Table 3.4, it reports that cultural industries do not affect unemployment rates, and even if they did, they would affect them in the opposite direction to what was hypothesized. Clearly, therefore, the findings in Table 3.4 are robust.

Table D3 Unemployment rate in the 22 Dutch metropolitan areas (1996- 2007), explained by the employment shares in the advanced producer services, the hotel and catering industry, and the cultural industries (multilevel regression analysis; entries are regression coefficients; estimation: maximum likelihood)

	Model 1	Model 2
Independents	*B*	*B*
Constant	16.77**	15.81***
Advanced producer services	-0.37***	-0.38***
Hotel and catering industry	-0.11	-0.13
Cultural industries		0.29
Controls		
Age 15-24	-0.18**	-0.18**
Variance metropolitan level ($N = 22$)	2.37	2.32
Variance year level ($N = 12$)	1.61	1.61
Log likelihood	-536.45	-535.90

Source: StatLine CBS (own calculations)
*$p < 0.05$; **$p < 0.01$; ***$p < 0.001$

Robustness checks on the findings in Table 5.1

Table D4 replicates the analysis in Table 5.1 on the impact of the producer services and immigrant shares on the unemployment rate of less-educated urbanites, and yields similar results. Just like Table 5.1, it indicates that the unemployment rate is the highest in cities with the highest immigrant shares, as predicted by the substitution thesis. Table D4 also replicates the most salient finding of Table 5.1: the employment share in the advanced producer services moderates that substitution effect. This is why Figure D2 is very similar to Figure 5.1, although the predicted unemployment rates are higher in the former than in the latter. This is in line with the previously mentioned underestimation of the unemployment rate among the less educated by *unemployment rate less educated.*

The robustness check in Table D4 is the last in this study, as Table 5.1 is the final one to analyse the causes of the varying unemployment rates among the less educated across Dutch cities. All robustness checks in this appendix yielded similar results to the findings they replicated, and they all did so in a similar and expected fashion: they demonstrated somewhat higher unemployment rates. Overall, it therefore seems safe to conclude that, despite the underestimation of what it aims to measure, i.e. the unemployment rates of the less educated across Dutch cities, all the analyses in Chapters 3 and 5 involving *unemployment rate less educated* did produce

Table D4 Unemployment rate in the 22 Dutch metropolitan areas (1998-2007), explained by the employment shares in the advanced producer services, the hotel and catering industry, the cultural industries, and immigrant shares (multilevel regression analysis; entries are regression coefficients; estimation: maximum likelihood)

	Model 1	Model 2	Model 3
Independents	*B*	*B*	*B*
Constant	6.20**	5.48**	-2.07
Advanced producer services	-0.16*	0.18**	0.14
Cultural industries	0.56*	0.43	0.53*
Hotel and catering industry	0.85**	0.55	0.62*
Immigrant share		0.12***	0.47***
Advanced producer services * immigrant share			-0.02**
Controls			
Age 15-24	-0.16**	-0.13*	-0.11
Variance metropolitan level (*N* = 22)	1.81	1.81	1.74
Variance year level (*N* = 10)	1.38	1.33	1.32
Log likelihood	-414.59	-408.32	-404.92

Source: StatLine CBS (own calculations)
*$p < 0.05$; **$p < 0.01$; ***$p < 0.001$

reliable results when it comes to the rejection and corroboration of the hypotheses tested. The polarization thesis, the substitution thesis, and the argument developed by means of the combination of the two stand the test for the Dutch case. On the other hand, the professionalization thesis and the consumerist explanation for varying unemployment rates among cities do not.

Figure D2 Unemployment rate of urbanites as predicted by the employment shares in the advanced producer services in the 22 Dutch metropolitan areas, if the immigrant share is 8% (dotted line) and 37% (solid line)

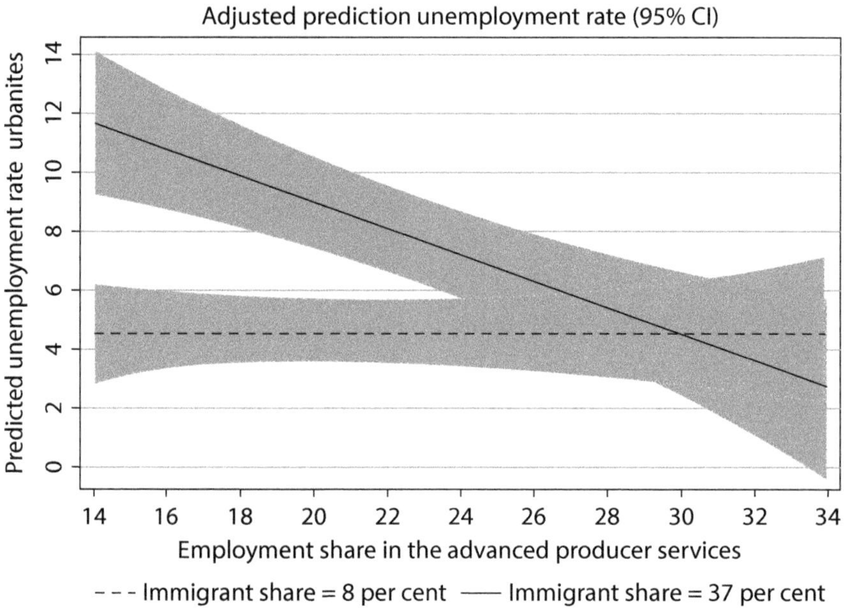

Literature

Alderson, A.S. (1999). Explaining deindustrialization: Globalization, failure, or success? *American Sociological Review, 64*(5), 701-721.

Alderson, A.S. & Beckfield, J. (2004). Power and position in the world city system. *American Journal of Sociology, 109*(4), 811-851.

Altonji, J.G. & Card, D. (1991). The effects of immigration on the labour market outcomes of less skilled natives. In J.M. Abowd & R.B. Freeman (eds.), *Immigration, trade, and the labour market* (pp. 201-34). Chicago: University of Chicago Press.

Amen, M.M., Archer, K. & Bosman. M.M. (eds.) (2006). *Relocating global cities: From the center to the margins*. Lanham: Rowan & Littlefield Publishers.

Aoyama, Y. (2009). Introduction – Consumption-centered research for diverse urban economies. *Urban Geography 30*(4), 341-343.

Aroca, P. & Maloney, W.F. (2005). Migration, trade and foreign direct investment in Mexico. *World Bank Economic Review 19*(3), 449-472.

Arrasco, R., Jimeno, J.F. & Ortega, A.C. (2008). The effect of immigration on the labour market performance of native-born workers: Some evidence for Spain. *Journal of Population Economics 21*(3), 627-648.

Asheim, B. & Hansen, H.K. (2009). Knowledge bases, talents, and contexts: On the usefulness of the creative class approach in Sweden. *Economic Geography 85*(4), 425-442.

Bailey, T. & Waldinger, R. (1991). The changing ethnic/racial division of labour. In J. Mollenkopf & M. Castells (eds.), *Dual city: Restructuring New York* (pp. 43-78). New York: Russell Sage Foundation.

Baimbridge, M., Burkitt, B. & Macey, M. (1994). The Maastricht treaty: Exacerbating racism in Europe? *Ethnic and Racial Studies 17*(3), 420-441.

Baum, S. (1997). Sydney, Australia: A global city? Testing the social polarisation thesis. *Urban Studies 34*(11), 1881-1901.

Baum, S. (1999). Social transformations in the global city: Singapore. *Urban Studies 36*(7), 1095-1117.

Beaverstock, J.V., Smith, R.G. & Taylor, P.J. (1999). A roster of world cities. *Cities 16*(6), 445-458.

Beer, A. & Forster, C. (2002). Global restructuring, the welfare state and urban programmes: Federal policies and inequality within Australian cities. *European Planning Studies 10*(1), 7-25.

Benton-Short, L., Price, M.D. & Friedman, S. (2005). Globalization from below: The ranking of global immigrant cities. *International Journal of Urban and Regional Research 29*(4), 945-959.

Black, W.K. (2009). How the servant became a predator: Finance's five fatal flaws. *Huffington Post*, October 12. Retrieved 31-12-2013, from www.huffingtonpost.com/william-k-black/how-the-servant-became-a_b_318010.html.

Borel-Saladin, J. & Crankshaw, O. (2009). Social polarisation or professionalisation? Another look at theory and evidence on deindustrialisation and the rise of the service sector. *Urban Studies 46*(3), 645-664.

Borges, J.L. (1975). *A Universal History of Infamy*. London: Penguin Books.

Borjas, G.J. (2006). Native internal migration and the labour market impact of immigration. *Journal of Human Resources 41*(2), 221-258.

Boubtane, E., Coulibaly, D. & Rault, C. (2013). Immigration, unemployment and GDP in the host country: Bootstrap panel granger causality analysis on OECD countries. *Economic Modelling 33*(C), 261-269.

Boustan, L.P., Baum-Snow, N., Black, S., Borjas, G.J., Card, D., Collins, W.J., Margo, R.A., Cutler, D.M. & Glaeser, E.L. (2007). Black migration, white flight: The effect of black migration on Northern cities and labour markets. *The Journal of Economic History 67*(2), 484-487.

Brady, D., Beckfield, J. & Zhao, W. (2007). The consequences of economic globalization for affluent democracies. *Annual Review of Sociology 33*, 313-334.

Bratsberg, B. & Raaum, O. (2012). Immigration and wages: Evidence from construction. *Economic Journal 122*(565), 1177-1205.

Braudel, F. (1984). *The perspective of the world*. London: Collins.

Braverman, H. (1974). *Labor and monopoly capital: The degradation of work in the twentieth century*. New York: Monthly Review Press.

Brenner, N. & Keil, R. (eds.) (2006). *The global cities reader*. Oxon / New York: Routledge.

Buck, N. (1997). Social divisions and labour market change in London. *Working Paper of the ESRC Research Centre on Micro-Social Change* No. 97-25.

Burgers, J. (1996). No polarisation in Dutch cities? Inequality in a corporatist country. *Urban Studies 33*(1), 99-105.

Burgers, J. & Musterd, S. (2001). Global and local determinants of social exclusion; Amsterdam versus Rotterdam. In H.T. Andersen & R. van Kempen (eds.), *Governing European cities: Social fragmentation, social exclusion and urban governance* (pp. 125-149). Aldershot: Ashgate.

Burgers, J. & Musterd, S. (2002). Understanding urban inequality: A model based on existing theories and an empirical illustration. *International Journal of Urban and Regional Research 26*(2), 403-413.

Card, D. (1990). The impact of the Mariel boatlift on the Miami labour market. *Industrial and Labour Relations Review 4*(2), 245-257.

Card, D. (2005). Is the new immigration really so bad? *NBER working Paper* No. 11547.

Catanzarite, L. (2003). Race-gender composition and occupational pay degradation. *Social Problems 50*(1), 14-37.

Catanzarite, L. & Aguilera, M.B. (2002). Working with co-ethnics: Earnings penalties for Latino immigrants at Latino jobsites. *Social Problems 49*(1), 101-127.

Cheshire, P. (1990). Explaining the recent performance of the European community's major urban regions. *Urban Studies 27*(3), 311-333.

Chiswick, B.R. (1982). The impact of immigration on the level and distribution of economic well-being. In B.R. Chiswick (ed.), *The gateway: Us immigration issues and policies* (pp. 289-313). Washington, DC: American Enterprise Institute for Public Policy Research.

Chiu, S.W.K. & Lui, T-L. (2004). Testing the global city-social polarisation thesis: Hong Kong since the 1990s. *Urban Studies 41*(10), 1863-1888.

Christophers, B. (2011). Revisiting the urbanization of capital. *Annals of the Association of American Geographers 101*(6), 1347-1364

Clark, T.N. (2003a). Introduction: Taking entertainment seriously. *Research in Urban Policy 9*, 1-17.

Clark, T.N. (2003b). Urban amenities: Lakes, opera, and juice bars: Do they drive development? *Research in Urban Policy 9*, 103-140.

Clark, T.N., Lloyd, R., Wong, K.K. & Jain, P. (2003). Amenities drive urban growth: A new paradigm and policy linkages. *Research in Urban Policy 9*, 291-322.

Cohen-Goldner, S. & Paserman, M.D. (2006). Mass migration to Israel and natives' employment transitions. *Industrial and Labour Relations Review 59*(4), 630-652.

Cox, R. & Watt, P. (2002). Globalization, polarization and the informal sector: The case of paid domestic workers in London. *Area 34*(1), 39-47.

Crankshaw, O. (2012). Deindustrialization, professionalization and racial inequality in Cape Town. *Urban Affairs Review 48*(6), 836-862.

Crankshaw, O & Borel-Saladin, J. (2014). Does deindustrialisation cause social polarisation in global cities? *Environment and Planning A 46*(8), 1852-1872.
Crinò, R. (2009). Offshoring, multinationals and labour market: A review of the empirical literature. *Journal of Economic Surveys 23*(1), 197-249.
Currid, E. (2009). Bohemia as subculture; 'Bohemia' as industry. Art, culture, and economic development. *Journal of Planning Literature 23*(4), 368-382.
Currid, E. (2010). Symposium introduction – Art and economic development: New directions for the growth of cities and regions. *Journal of Planning Education and Research 29*(3), 257-261.
Currid, E. & Connolly, J. (2008). Patterns of knowledge: The geography of advanced services and the case of art and culture. *Annals of the Association of American Geographers 98*(2), 414-434.
Currid-Halkett, E. & Stolarick, K. (2013). Baptism by fire: Did the creative class generate economic growth during the crisis. *Cambridge Journal of Regions, Economy and Society 6*(1), 55-69.

Daly, M.T. & Stimson, R. (1992). Sydney: Australia's gateway and financial capital. In E. Blakely, and T.J. Stimpson (eds.), *New cities of the Pacific Rim* (pp.18.1-18.42). Berkeley: University of California, Institute for Urban and Regional Development.
Damette, O. & Fromentin, V. (2013). Migration and labour markets in OECD countries: A panel cointegration approach. *Applied Economics 45*(16), 2295-2304.
Dangschat, J.S. (1994). Concentration of poverty in the landscapes of 'boomtown' Hamburg: The creation of a new urban underclass. *Urban Studies 31*(7), 1133-1147.
De Koster, W., Achterberg, P. & Van der Waal, J. (2013). The new right and the welfare state: On the electoral relevance of welfare chauvinism and welfare populism in the Netherlands. *International Political Science Review 34*(1), 3-20.
De Koster, W., Achterberg, P., Van der Waal, J., Van Bohemen, S. & Kemmers, R. (2014). Progressiveness and the new right: The electoral relevance of culturally progressive values in the Netherlands. *West European Politics 37*(3), 584-604.
De Koster, W. & Van der Waal, J. (2014). Botsende opvattingen over etnische diversiteit en sociale orde: Hoe verschillen tussen lager- en hogeropgeleiden te verklaren? [Colliding views on ethnic diversity and social order: How to explain the educational divide?]. In: M. Bovens, P. Dekker & W. Tiemijer (eds.), *Gescheiden werelden? Een verkenning van sociaal-culturele tegenstellingen in Nederland* (pp.165-90). The Hague: SCP/WRR.
Derudder, B., Taylor, P.J., Witlox, F. & Catalano, G. (2003). Hierarchical tendencies and regional patterns in the world city network: A global urban analysis of 234 cities. *Regional Studies 37*(9), 875-886.
Derudder, B. & Taylor, P.J. (2005). The cliquishness of world cities. *Global Networks 5*(1), 71-91.
Doogan, K. (2009). *New capitalism. The transformation of work*. Cambridge: Polity Press.

Elliott, J.R. (1999a). Putting 'global cities' in their place: Urban hierarchy and low-income employment during the post-war era. *Urban Geography 20*(1), 95-115.
Elliott, J.R. (1999b). Urban restructuring revisited: Organizational and labor market changes during the 1980s. *Sociological Perspectives 42*(3), 421-438.
Elliott, J.R. (2004). The work of cities: Underemployment and urban change in late-20th-century America. *Cityscape 7*(1), 107-133.
Ellis, M. & Wright, R. (1999). The industrial division of labour among immigrants and internal migrants to the Los Angeles economy. *International Migration Review 33*(1), 26-54.
Esping-Andersen, G. (1993). *Changing classes. Stratification and mobility in post-industrial societies*. London: Sage.

Esping-Andersen, G. (1999). *Social foundations of postindustrial economies*. Oxford: Oxford University Press.

Fainstein, S. (2002). Inequality in global city regions. In A.J. Scott (ed.), *Global city regions. Trends, theory, policy* (pp. 285-298). Oxford: Oxford University Press.

Fainstein, S., Gordon, I. & Harloe, M. (eds.) (1992). *Divided cities: New York and London in the contemporary world*. Oxford: Blackwell Publishers.

Faux, J. (2006). *The global class war: How America's bipartisan elite lost our future and what it will take to win it back*. Hoboken: Wiley.

Feenstra, R.C. (2007). Globalization and its impact on labour. *WIIW Working Papers* No. 44.

Ferderman, M.N., Harrington, D.E. & Krynski, K.J. (2006). Vietnamese manicurists: Are immigrants displacing natives or finding new nails to polish? *Industrial & Labour Relations Review* 59(2), 302-318.

Florida, R. (2002). Bohemia and economic geography. *Journal of Economic Geography* 2(1), 55-71.

Florida, R. (2003). Cities and the creative class. *City & Community* 2(1), 3-19.

Florida, R. (2004). *The rise of the creative class: And how it's transforming work, leisure, community and everyday life*. New York: Basic Books.

Florida, R. (2005). *Cities and the creative class*. New York: Routledge.

Florida, R. (2010). *The great reset. How new ways of living and working drive post-crash prosperity*. New York: HarperCollins.

Florida, R., Mellander, C. & Stolarick, K. (2008). Inside the black box of regional development: Human capital, the creative class and tolerance. *Journal of Economic Geography* 8(5), 615-649.

Friedberg, R.M. & Hunt, J. (1995). The impact of immigrants on host country wages, employment and growth. *Journal of Economic Perspectives* 9(2), 23-44.

Friedmann, J. (1986). The world city hypothesis. *Development and Change* 17(1), 69-83.

Friedmann, J. (1995). Where we stand now. A decade of world city research. In P.L. Knox & P.J. Taylor (eds.), *World cities in a world-system* (pp. 21-47). Cambridge: Cambridge University Press.

Friedmann, J. (2001). World cities revisited: A comment. *Urban Studies* 38(13), 2535-2536.

Friedmann, J. & Wolff, G. (1982). World city formation: An agenda for research and action. *International Journal of Urban and Regional Research* 6(3), 309-344.

Fujita, M. & Thisse, J-J. (2002). *Economics of agglomeration. Cities, industrial location, and regional growth*. Cambridge: Cambridge University Press.

Glaeser, E.L. (2009). How some places fare better in hard times. *New York Times*, March 24. Retrieved 30-12-2013, from http://economix.blogs.nytimes.com/2009/03/17/why-is-new-yorks-unemployment-rate-relatively-low/.

Glaeser, E.L. (2011). *Triumph of the city. How our greatest invention makes us richer, smarter, greener, healthier, and happier*. New York: The Penguin Press.

Glaeser, E.L., Kolko, J. & Saiz, A. (2001). Consumer city. *Journal of Economic Geography* 1(1), 27-50.

Glaeser, E.L., Kolko, J. & Saiz, A. (2003). Consumers and cities. *Research in Urban Policy* 9, 177-183.

Glitz, A. (2012). The labor market impact of immigration: A quasi-experiment exploiting immigrant location rules in Germany. *Journal of Labor Economics* 30(1), 175-213.

Gordon, I. & Sassen, S. (1992). Restructuring the urban labour markets. In S. Fainstein, I. Gordon & M. Harloe (eds.), *Divided cities. New York and London in the contemporary world* (pp. 105-58). Oxford: Blackwell.

Gouldner, A.W. (1970). *The coming crisis of Western sociology*. London: Heinemann.

Grabher, G. & Powell, W.W. (eds.) (2004). *Networks*. Cheltenham: Edward Elgar.

Grodach, C. (2013). Cultural economy planning in creative cities: Discourse and practice. *International Journal of Urban and Regional Research 37*(5), 1747-1765.

Hamnett, C. (1994a). Social polarisation in global cities: Theory and evidence. *Urban Studies 31*(3), 401-425.
Hamnett, C. (1994b). Socio-economic change in London: Professionalization not polarization. *Built Environment 20*(2), 192-203.
Hamnett, C. (1996a). Social polarisation, economic restructuring and welfare state regimes. *Urban Studies 33*(8), 1407-1430.
Hamnett, C. (1996b). Why Sassen is wrong: A response to Burgers. *Urban Studies 33*(1), 107-110.
Hamnett, C. (2004). *Unequal city. London in the global arena.* London: Routledge.
Hamnett, C. & Cross, D. (1998). Social polarisation and inequality in London: The earnings evidence, 1979-95. *Environment and Planning C - Government & Policy 16*(6), 659-680.
Hayase, Y. (2001). Japanese foreign direct investment, employment, and international migration in East Asia. *Asian and Pacific Migration Journal 10*(3-4), 535-558.
Hijzen, A. & Swaim, P. (2007). Does offshoring reduce industry employment? *National Institute Economic-Review 201*(1), 86-96.
Himmelfarb, G. (1949). The American revolution in the political theory of Lord Acton. *Journal of Modern History 21*(4), 293-312.
Hoyler, M., Kloosterman, R. & Sokol, M. (2008). Polycentric puzzles – Emerging mega-city regions seen through the lens of advanced producer services. *Regional Studies 42*(8), 1055-1064.
Hoyman, M. & Faricy, C. (2009). It takes a village: A test of the creative class, social capital, and human capital theories. *Urban Affairs Review 44*(3), 311-333.
Hox, J.J. (1995). *Applied multilevel statistics.* Amsterdam: TT-Publications.

Indergaard, M., Pratt, A.C. & Hutton, T.A. (2013). Creative cities after the fall of finance. *Cities* 33, 1-4.
INDIAC. (2009). *Monitor kennismigrantenregeling 2008.* Retrieved 25-11-2009, from www.ind.nl/nl/Images/12.%20eindrapport%20Monitor%20Kennismigranten%202008%20-%20v%2006%20-%20naar%20repro%20090311%20DEF_tcm5-183778.pdf.
Islam, A. (2009). The substitutability of labour between immigrants and natives in the Canadian labour market circa 1995. *Journal of Population Economics 22*(1), 199-217.
Islam, A. & Fausten, D. (2008). Skilled immigration and wages in Australia. *Economic Record 84*(1), 66-82.
Iversen, T. & Cusack, T.R. (2000). The causes of welfare state expansion: Deindustrialization or globalization. *World Politics 52*(2), 313-349.

Jarvorcik, B., Özden, C., Spatareau, M. & Neagu, C. (2011). Migrant networks and foreign direct investments. *Journal of Development Economics 94*(2), 231-241.
Jean, S. & Jimenez, M. (2007). The unemployment impact of immigration in OECD countries. *OECD Economics Department Working Papers* No. 563.
Johnson, G.E. (1980). The labour market effects of immigration. *Industrial and Labour Relations Review 33*(3), 331-341.

Kasarda, J.D. (1985). Urban change and minority opportunities. In P.E. Peterson (ed.), *The new urban reality* (pp. 33-67). Washington, DC: Brookings.
Kasarda, J.D. & Friedrichs, J. (1985). Comparative demographic-employment mismatches in U.S. and West German cities. *Research in the Sociology of Work 3*(1), 1-30.

Kasarda, J.D. & Friedrichs, J. (1986). Economic transformation, minorities, and urban demographic-employment mismatch in the U.S. and West Germany. In H.J. Ewers, J.B. Goddard & H. Matzerath (eds.), *The future of the metropolis. Berlin, London, Paris, New York: Economic aspects* (pp. 221-249). Berlin/New York: Walter de Gruyter.

Keil, R. & Ronneberger, K. (1992). Going up the country: Internationalization and urbanization on Frankfurt's northern fringe. Paper presented at the UCLA International Sociological Association, Research Committee 29, *A new urban and regional hierarchy? Impacts of modernization, restructuring and the end of bipolarity*: April 24-6, Los Angeles, United States.

Kloosterman, R.C. (1996). Double Dutch: Polarization trends in Amsterdam and Rotterdam. *Regional Studies 30*(5), 467-476.

Knapp, W. & Schmitt, P. (2008). Discourse on 'metropolitan driving forces' and 'uneven development': Germany and the RhineRuhr conurbation. *Regional Studies 42*(8), 1187-1204.

Kollmeyer, C. (2009). Explaining deindustrialization: How affluence, productivity growth, and globalization diminish manufacturing employment. *American Journal of Sociology 114*(6), 1644-1674.

Kreft, I. & De Leeuw, J. (1998). *Introducing multilevel modeling*. London: Sage Publications.

Krugman, P. (1994). *Peddling prosperity: Economic sense and nonsense in the age of diminished expectations*. New York: Norton.

Krugman, P. (1996). *Pop internationalism*. Cambridge: The MIT Press.

Krugman, P. & Lawrence, R.Z. (1993). Trade, jobs and wages. *NBER Working Paper* No. 4478.

Kugler, M. & Rapoport, H. (2007). International labor and capital flows: Complements or substitutes? *Economics Letters 94*(1), 155-162.

Leblang, D. (2010). Familiarity breeds investments: Diaspora networks and international investment. *American Political Science Review 104*(3), 584-600.

Lemanski, C. (2007). Global cities in the South: Deepening social and spatial polarisation in Cape Town. *Cities 24*(6), 448-461.

Leonardt, D. (2009). After the great recession. *New York Times*, April 28. Retrieved 31-12-2013, from www.nytimes.com/2009/05/03/magazine/03Obama-t.html?pagewanted=1&_r=2&partner=rss&emc=rss&.

Levine, M.V. (1990). *The reconquest of Montreal. Language policy and social change in a bilingual city*. Philadelphia: Temple University Press.

Longhi, S., Nijkamp, P. & Poot, J. (2005). A meta-analytic assessment of the effect of immigration on wages. *Journal of Economic Surveys 19*(3), 451-477.

MacLachlan, I. & Sawada, R. (1997). Measures of income inequality and social polarization in Canadian metropolitan areas. *Canadian Geographer 41*(4), 377-397.

Malecki, E.J. & Ewers, M.C. (2007). Labor migration to world cities: With a research agenda for the Arab Gulf. *Progress in Human Geography 31*(4), 467-484.

Maloutas, T. (2007). Segregation, social polarization and immigration in Athens during the 1990s: Theoretical expectations and contextual difference. *International Journal of Urban and Regional Research 31*(4), 733-758.

Markusen, A. & Schrock, G. (2009). Consumption-driven urban development. *Urban Geography 30*(4), 344-367.

Markusen, A. & Schrock, G. (2006). The artistic dividend: Urban artistic specialisation and economic development implications. *Urban Studies 43*(10), 1661-1686.

Massey, D.S. (1988). Development and international migration in comparative perspective. *Population and Development Review 14*(3), 383-413.

May, J., Wills, J., Datta, K., Evans, Y., Herbert, J. & McIlwaine, C. (2007). Keeping London working: Global cities, the British state and London's new migrant division of labour. *Transactions of the Institute of British Geographers 32*(1), 151-167.

Meijer, M. (1993). Growth and decline of European cities: Changing positions of cities in Europe. *Urban Studies 30*(6), 981-990.

Merton, R.K. (1959). *Social Theory and social structure*. 3rd edition. Glencoe: Free Press.

Ministry of Economic Affairs (2004). *Pieken in de delta: Gebiedsgerichte economische perspectieven* [*Peaks in the Delta: Regional economic perspectives*]. The Hague: Ministry of Economic Affairs.

Mollenkopf, J. (2009). The Dutch orange and the big apple: A comparative commentary. In J.W. Duyvendak, F. Hendriks & M. van Niekerk (eds.), *City in sight. Dutch dealings with urban change* (pp. 267-276). Amsterdam: Amsterdam University Press.

Mollenkopf, J. & Castells, M. (eds.) (1992). *Dual city: Restructuring New York*. New York: Russell Sage Foundation.

Molnar, M., Pain, N. & Taglioni, D. (2007). The internationalisation of production, international outsourcing and employment in the OECD. *OECD Economics Department Working Papers* No. 561.

Musterd, S. & Kovacs, Z. (eds.) (2013). *Place making and policies for competitive cities*. Oxford: Wiley-Blackwell.

Musterd, S. & Murie, A. (eds.) (2010). *Making competitive cities*. Oxford: Wiley-Blackwell.

Musterd, S., Ostendorf, W. & Breebaart, M. (1998). *Multi-ethnic metropolis: Patterns and policies*. Kluwer: Dordrecht.

Myers, R.H. (1990). *Classical and modern regression with applications*. 2nd edition. Belmont: Duxbury Press.

Neal, Z. (2008). The duality of world cities and firms: Comparing networks, hierarchies, and inequalities in the global economy. *Global Networks 8*(1), 94-115.

Neal, Z. (2012). Creative employment and jet set cities: Disentangling causal effects. *Urban Studies 49*(12), 2693-2709.

Newman, P. & Thornley, A. (1996). *Urban planning in Europe: International competition, national systems and planning projects*. London/New York: Routledge.

Norgaard, H. (2003). The global city thesis – Social polarization and changes in the distribution of wages. *Geografiska Annaler. Series B. Human Geography 85*(5), 103-119.

Noyelle, T.J. (1983). The rise of advanced services: Some implications for economic development in U.S. Cities. *Journal of the American Planning Association 49*(3), 280-290.

OECD (2007). OECD workers in the global economy: Increasing vulnerable? In OECD, *OECD employment outlook 2007* (pp. 105-155). Paris: OECD Publishing.

Okkerse, L. (2008). How to measure labour market effects of immigration: A review. *Journal of Economic Surveys 22*(1), 1-30.

Onaran, Ö. (2012). The effect of foreign affiliate employment on wages, employment, and the wage share in Austria. *Review of Political Economy 24*(2), 251-271.

Parkinson, M., Foley, B. & Judd, D. (eds.) 1988. *Regenerating the cities: The UK crisis and the US experience*. Manchester: Manchester University Press.

Porter, M.E. (1998). Clusters and the new economics of competition. *Harvard Business Review 76*(6), 77-90.

Portes, A. (2000). Immigration and the metropolis: Reflections on urban history. *Journal of International Migration and Integration 1*(2), 153-157.

Portes, A. & Sassen-Koob, S. (1987). Making it underground: comparative material on the informal sector in Western market economies. *American Journal of Sociology 93*(1), 30-61.
Pratschke, J. & Morliccho, E. (2012). Social polarisation, the labour market and economic restructuring in Europe: An urban perspective. *Urban Studies 49*(4), 1891-1907.

Rath, J. (ed.) (2000). *Immigrant businesses: The economic, political and social environment.* Houndsmills: MacMillan Press.
Reed, D. & Danziger, S. (2007). Globalization and economic outcomes for minority groups – The effects of recent immigration on racial/ethnic labour market differentials. *American Economic Review 97*(2), 373-377.
Rhein, C. (1996). Social segmentation and spatial polarisation in greater Paris. In J. O'Loughlin and J. Friedrichs (eds.), *Social polarisation in post-industrial metropolises* (pp. 45-70). Berlin/ New York: Walter de Gruyter.
Ricketts, E. (1987). U.S. investment and immigration from the Caribbean. *Social Problems 34*(4), 374-387.
Rowthorn, R. & Ramaswamy, R. (1997). Deindustrialization: Causes and implications. *International Monetary Fund Working Paper* No. 42.
Rowthorn, R. & Ramaswamy, R. (1999). Growth, trade, and deindustrialization. *International Monetary Fund Staff Papers* No. 46.

Saeger, S.S. (1997). Globalization and deindustrialization: Myth and reality in the OECD. *Weltwirtschaftliches Archiv 133*(4), 579-608.
Sanderson, M.R. & Kentor, J. (2008). Foreign direct investment and international migration: A cross-national analysis of less-developed countries, 1985-2000. *International Sociology 23*(4), 514-539.
Samers, M. (2002). Immigration and the global city hypothesis: Towards an alternative research agenda. *International Journal of Urban and Regional Research 26*(2), 389-402.
Sassen, S. (1988). *The mobility of labor and capital. A study in international investment and labor flow.* Cambridge: Cambridge University Press.
Sassen, S. (1991). *The global city: New York, London, Tokyo.* 1st edition. Princeton: Princeton University Press.
Sassen, S. (1994). *Cities in a world economy.* 1st edition. London: Pine Forge Press.
Sassen, S. (1995). On concentration and centrality in the global city. In P.L. Knox & P.J. Taylor (eds.), *World cities in a world-system* (pp. 63-75). Cambridge: Cambridge University Press.
Sassen, S. (1998). *Globalization and its discontents.* New York: The New York Press.
Sassen, S. (2000). *Cities in a world economy.* 2nd edition. London: Pine Forge Press.
Sassen, S. (2001). *The global city: New York, London, Tokyo.* 2nd edition. Princeton: Princeton University Press.
Sassen, S. (2006a). *Cities in a world economy.* 3rd edition. Thousand Oaks: Pine Forge Press.
Sassen, S. (2006b). Foreign investment: A neglected variable. In A.M. Messina & G. Lahav (eds.), *The migration reader: Exploring politics and policy* (pp. 596-608). Boulder: Lynne Rienner Publishers.
Sassen, S. (2006c). Foreword: Searching for the global in the urban. In M.M. Amen, K. Archer & M.M. Bosman, *Relocating global cities: From the center to the margins* (pp. ix-xiii). Lanham: Rowman & Littlefield Publishers.
Sassen, S. (2006d). *Territory, authority, rights: From medieval to global assemblages.* Princeton: Princeton University Press.
Sassen, S. (2007). *A sociology of globalization.* New York: W.W. Norton & Company.
Sassen, S. (2012). *Cities in a world economy.* 4th edition. Thousand Oaks: Pine Forge Press.

Sassen-Koob, S. (1984a). Direct foreign investment: A migration push-factor. *Environment and Planning C* 2(4), 399-416.
Sassen-Koob, S. (1984b). The new labor demand in global cities. In M.P. Smith (ed.), *Cities in transformation: Capital, class and the state* (pp. 139-171). Beverly Hills: Sage.
Sassen-Koob, S. (1985). Capital mobility and labor migration: Their expression in core cities. In M. Timberlake (ed.), *Urbanization in the world economy* (pp. 231-265). Orlando: Academic Press.
Sassen-Koob, S. (1986). New York City: Economic restructuring and immigration. *Development and change* 17(2), 85-119.
Scott, A.J. & Storper, M. (1986). *Production, work, territory: The geographical anatomy of industrial capitalism*. London: Allen & Unwin Publishers.
Smith, M.P. (ed.) (1984). *Cities in transformation. Class, capital, and the state*. Beverly Hills: Sage.
Smith, M.P. (1998). The global city – Whose social construct is it anyway? A comment on White. *Urban Affairs Review* 33(4), 482-488.
Smith, M.P. (2001). *Transnational urbanism. Locating globalization*. Malden: Blackwell.
Steijn, B., Snel, E. & Van der Laan, L. 2000. Een postindustriële klassenstructuur? Het klassenschema van Esping-Andersen toegepast op Nederland, Amsterdam en Rotterdam [A post-industrial class structure? Esping-Andersen's class scheme applied to the Netherlands, Amsterdam, and Rotterdam]. *Sociologische Gids* 58(1), 77-94.
Steinhardt, M.F. (2011). The wage impact of immigration in Germany – New evidence for skill groups and occupations. *BE Journal of Economic Analysis & Policy* 11(1), art. 31.
Storper, M. & Venables, A.J. (2004). Buzz: Face-to-face contact and the urban economy. *Journal of Economic Geography* 4(4), 351-370.

Tai, P.-F. (2006). Social polarisation: Comparing Singapore, Hong Kong and Taipei. *Urban Studies*, 43(10), 1737-1756.
Tai, P-F. (2010). Beyond 'social polarization'? A test for Asian world cities in developmental states. *International Journal of Urban and Regional Research* 34(4), 743-761.
Taylor, P.J. (2002). *Amsterdam in a world city network*. Retrieved 23-10-2008, from www.lboro.ac.uk/gawc/rb/rm1.pdf.
Taylor, P.J. (2004). *World city network: A global urban analysis*. London/New York: Routledge.
Taylor, P.J. & Aranya, R. (2008). A global 'urban roller coaster'? Connectivity changes in the world city network, 2000-2004. *Regional Studies* 42(1), 1-16.
Timberlake, M., Sanderson, M.R., Ma, X., Derudder, B., Winitsky, J. & Witlox, F. (2012). Testing a global city hypothesis: An assessment of polarization across U.S. cities. *City & Community* 11(1), 74-93.
Trachte, K. & Ross, R. (1985). The crisis of Detroit and the emergence of global capitalism. *International Journal of Urban and Regional Research* 9(1), 186-217.

Vaattovaara, M. & Kortteinen, M. (2003). Beyond polarisation versus professionalisation? A case study of the development of the Helsinki region, Finland. *Urban Studies* 40(11), 2127-2145.
Van der Waal, J. (2010). *Stedelijke economieën in een tijd van mondialisering. Arbeidsmarktkansen en etnocentrisme van laaggeschoolden in Nederlandse steden* [*Urban economies in an era of globalisation. Labour market opportunities and ethnocentrism in Dutch cities*]. Amsterdam: Amsterdam University Press.
Van der Waal, J. (2012). Post-industrialisation, immigration, and unemployment. How and why the impact of immigration on unemployment differs between Dutch cities. *Urban Studies* 49(8), 1711-1724.
Van der Waal, J. (2013a). Foreign direct investments and international migration to Dutch cities. *Urban Studies* 50(2), 293-310.

Van der Waal, J. (2013b). Cultural amenities and unemployment in Dutch cities. Disentangling a consumerist and productivist explanation for less-educated urbanites' varying unemployment levels across urban economies. *Urban Studies 50*(14), 2869-2885.

Van der Waal, J. (2013c). The impact of immigration on wages in Amsterdam and Rotterdam. In A. Mukherjee (ed.), *Wages and employment. Economics, structures, and gender differences* (pp. 147-166). New York: Nova Science Publishers, Inc.

Van der Waal, J. & Burgers, J. (2009). Unravelling the global city debate on social inequality: A firm-level analysis of wage inequality in Amsterdam and Rotterdam. *Urban Studies 46*(13), 2715-2729.

Vliegen, M. (2005). Grootstedelijke agglomeraties en stadsgewesten afgebakend [Metropolitan agglomerations and urban regions demarcated]. Voorburg/Heerlen: Centraal Bureau voor de Statistiek.

Waldinger, R. (1987). Changing ladders and musical chairs: Ethnicity and opportunity in post-industrial New York. *Politics & Society 15*(4), 369-401.

Waldinger, R. (1994). The making of an immigrant niche. *International Migration Review 28*(1), 3-30.

Waldinger, R. (1996). *Still the promised city? African-Americans and new immigrants in postindustrial New York*. Cambridge: Harvard University Press.

Walks, A.R. (2001). The social ecology of the post-Fordist/global city? Economic restructuring and socio-spatial polarisation in the Toronto urban region. *Urban Studies 38*(3), 407-447.

Wang, M., Sunny Wong, M.C. & Granato, J. (2013). The effect of foreign direct investment on international migration: Does education matter? *The World Economy 36*(5), 1-26.

Wessel, T. (2001). Losing control? Inequality and social divisions in Oslo. *European Planning Studies 9*(7), 889-906.

White, J.W. (1998). Old wine, cracked bottle? Tokyo, Paris and the global city hypothesis. *Urban Affairs Review 33*(4), 451-477.

Wilson, F.D. & Jaynes, G. (2000). Migration and the employment and wages of native and immigrant workers. *Work and Occupations 27*(1), 135-167.

Wojan, T.R., Lambert, D.M. & McGranahan, D.A. (2007). Emoting with their feet: Bohemian attraction to creative milieu. *Journal of Economic Geography 7*(6), 711-736.

Wood, A.P. (1994). *North-South trade, employment and inequality: Changing fortunes in a skill-driven world*. Oxford: Clarendon Press.

Wright, R. & Ellis, M. (1997). Nativity, ethnicity, and the evolution of the intra-urban division of labour in metropolitan Los Angeles, 1970-1990. *Urban Geography 18*(3), 243-263.

Wright, E.O. & Martin, B. (1987). The transformation of the American class structure, 1960-1980. *American Journal of Sociology 93*(1), 1-29.

Yang, P.Q. (1998). The demand for immigration to the United States. *Population and Environment: A Journal of Interdisciplinary Studies 19*(4), 357-383.

Zapkau, F.B. & Schwens, C. (2014). Foreign direct investments and domestic employment of German SME's: The moderating effect of owner management. *Journal of Small Business Management 52*(3), 451-476.

Zhong, X., Clark, T.N. & Sassen, S. (2007). Globalization, producer services, and income inequality across US metro areas. *International Review of Sociology 17*(3), 385-391.

Zorlu, A. & Hartog, J. (2005). The effect of immigration on wages in three European countries. *Journal of Population Economics 18*(1), 113-135.

Zorlu, A. & Mulder, C. (2008). Initial and subsequent location choices of immigrants to the Netherlands. *Regional Studies 42*(2): 245-264

Index

Index of names

Index of subjects

For Product Safety Concerns and Information please contact our EU representative GPSR@taylorandfrancis.com
Taylor & Francis Verlag GmbH, Kaufingerstraße 24, 80331 München, Germany

www.ingramcontent.com/pod-product-compliance
Ingram Content Group UK Ltd.
Pitfield, Milton Keynes, MK11 3LW, UK
UKHW022122190926
475702UK00013B/1603

* 9 7 8 1 0 4 1 1 8 8 0 1 8 *